SHOW OFF

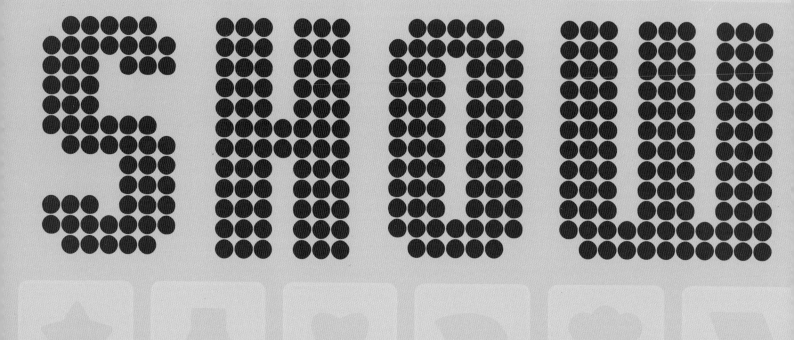

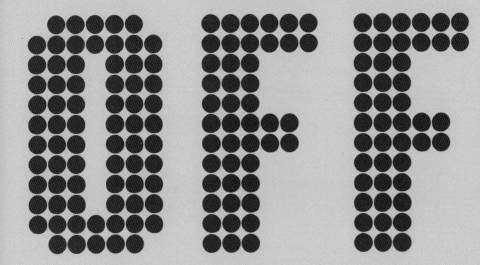

OFF

**How to Do
Absolutely Everything.
One Step at a Time.**

Sarah Hines Stephens
and Bethany Mann

CANDLEWICK PRESS

contents

• how to use this book

amaze

investigate

52 erupt a soda geyser
53 squeeze an egg into a bottle
54 bend water with static
55 ring a bell with a tv
56 light a room with a ponytail
57 make tissue defy gravity
58 tell time with a potato
59 mold a bouncy ball
60 grow a crystal initial
61 lift a friend's fingerprint
62 isolate dna
63 encode notes with a scytale
64 send secrets by morse code
65 spy with a periscope
66 write in invisible ink
67 turn the world upside down
68 spin a mini kaleidoscope
69 view an eclipse
70 make a sun print
71 get cooking in a solar oven
72 rig a lightbulb
73 trap shadows
74 light up a lava lamp
75 flash a matchbook light
76 build a tiny robot
77 set off an exploding volcano
78 launch a rocket

create

79 take aim with a catapult
80 fire a pen crossbow
81 design a kite
82 fly a kite
83 fold a paper airplane
84 whip out a ninja star
85 marbleize pretty paper
86 cut festive papel picado
87 paste up a piñata
88 light paper-bag luminarias
89 fill a sea globe
90 pour a sand candle
91 weave a friendship bracelet
92 hook a gum-wrapper chain
93 link a daisy chain
94 tie-dye a stripy shirt
95 tie-dye a swirly shirt
96 cover an mp3 player
97 roll up a duct-tape rose
98 bead charms
99 mold clay monsters

100 create silhouette portraits
101 draw a cat
102 sketch a dog
103 draft a horse
104 draw awesome manga
105 flip out with a flip book
106 pop out a 3-d card
107 sport a comic-book tote
108 beautify sneakers
109 punk up high-tops
110 trick out slip-ons
111 fashion a no-sew skirt
112 paint one-of-a-kind nails
113 make a crazy ponytail
114 ink a fake tattoo
115 annoy with a balloon horn
116 toot a straw horn
117 wire cereal-box speakers
118 screen-print a t-shirt
119 make a compact disc-o ball

explore

cook

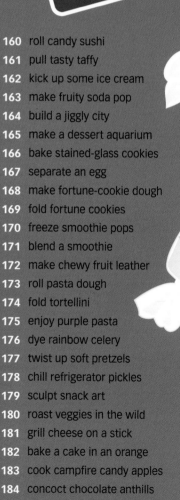

move

- tell me more
- index
- about the authors
- credits
- get involved!

how to use this book

Show Off is a brand-new type of book—one that uses pictures instead of words to show you how to do all sorts of activities. Sometimes, though, you may need a little extra info. In those cases, look to these symbols to help you out.

TOOLS The toolbar shows the ingredients you'll need to do most projects. Follow the steps to see the amount or measurement that you'll need of each ingredient.

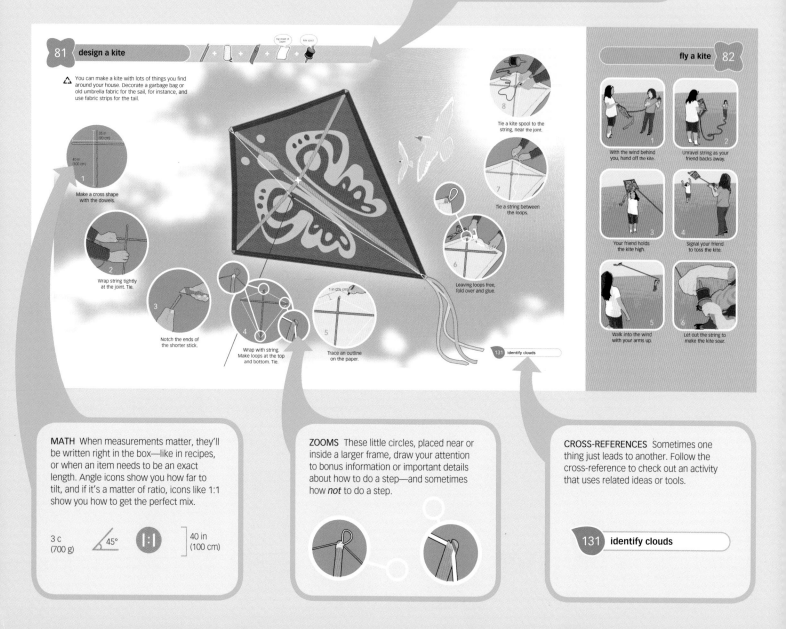

81 design a kite

⚠ You can make a kite with lots of things you find around your house. Decorate a garbage bag or old umbrella fabric for the sail, for instance, and use fabric strips for the tail.

1 Make a cross shape with the dowels.

2 Wrap string tightly at the joint. Tie.

3 Notch the ends of the shorter stick.

4 Wrap with string. Make loops at the top and bottom. Tie.

5 Trace an outline on the paper.

6 Leaving loops free, fold over and glue.

7 Tie a string between the loops.

8 Tie a kite spool to the string, near the joint.

131 identify clouds

fly a kite 82

1 With the wind behind you, hand off the kite.

2 Unravel string as your friend backs away.

3 Your friend holds the kite high.

4 Signal your friend to toss the kite.

5 Walk into the wind with your arms up.

6 Let out the string to make the kite soar.

MATH When measurements matter, they'll be written right in the box—like in recipes, or when an item needs to be an exact length. Angle icons show you how far to tilt, and if it's a matter of ratio, icons like 1:1 show you how to get the perfect mix.

3 c (700 g)   45°   1:1   40 in (100 cm)

ZOOMS These little circles, placed near or inside a larger frame, draw your attention to bonus information or important details about how to do a step—and sometimes how *not* to do a step.

CROSS-REFERENCES Sometimes one thing just leads to another. Follow the cross-reference to check out an activity that uses related ideas or tools.

131 identify clouds

a word to parents

The activities in this book are designed for children ages ten and older. While we have made every effort to ensure that the information in this book is accurate, reliable, and totally cool, please assess your own child's suitability for a particular activity before allowing him or her to attempt it, and provide adult supervision as appropriate. We disclaim all liability for any unintended, unforeseen, or improper application of the suggestions featured in this book. We will, however, be happy to accept the credit for increased awesomeness.

tool kit

Here are some basic items that you probably have at home, so they aren't listed in the toolbars. Pack a **Show Off** tool kit, and keep it handy!

scissors

glue

pen, pencil, and marker

plain paper

tape

utensils

water

containers

symbols

tell me more	Flip to the back of the book for extra info about this activity, including trivia, special techniques, history, or the science that makes it all happen.
uses recyclables	This project helps you recycle old junk you probably have at your house. Go green!
messy	Wear old clothes, put down newspapers, and warn the parents. This one will be messy!
science project	This activity makes for a great school project, or a fun way to learn about basic scientific principles.
see our Web site	For additional resources—art, templates, late-breaking information, and more—follow this icon to our Web site, www.showoffbook.com.
15 min	The timer shows the number of hours, minutes, or seconds you should spend doing a step.
	The thermometer indicates the temperature to which you should heat or cool an ingredient.
×2	This symbol tells the number of times you should repeat a particular action.
	The calendar's x's shows the number of days, weeks, or months that a step requires.
*	Follow the little asterisk in a step to the larger one on the page for information about alternative methods or materials, or for tips.

amaze

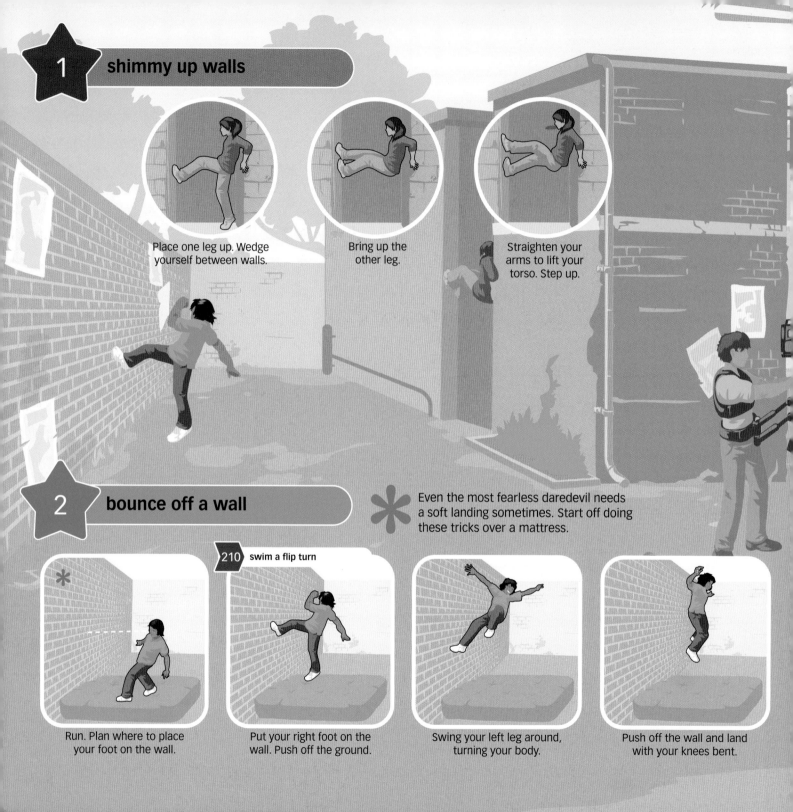

1 shimmy up walls

Place one leg up. Wedge yourself between walls.

Bring up the other leg.

Straighten your arms to lift your torso. Step up.

2 bounce off a wall

Even the most fearless daredevil needs a soft landing sometimes. Start off doing these tricks over a mattress.

210 swim a flip turn

Run. Plan where to place your foot on the wall.

Put your right foot on the wall. Push off the ground.

Swing your left leg around, turning your body.

Push off the wall and land with your knees bent.

do a stuntman vault 3

Get a running start.

Plant your hand, then jump off the ground.

Swing your legs up and over.

Keep your knees loose as you land.

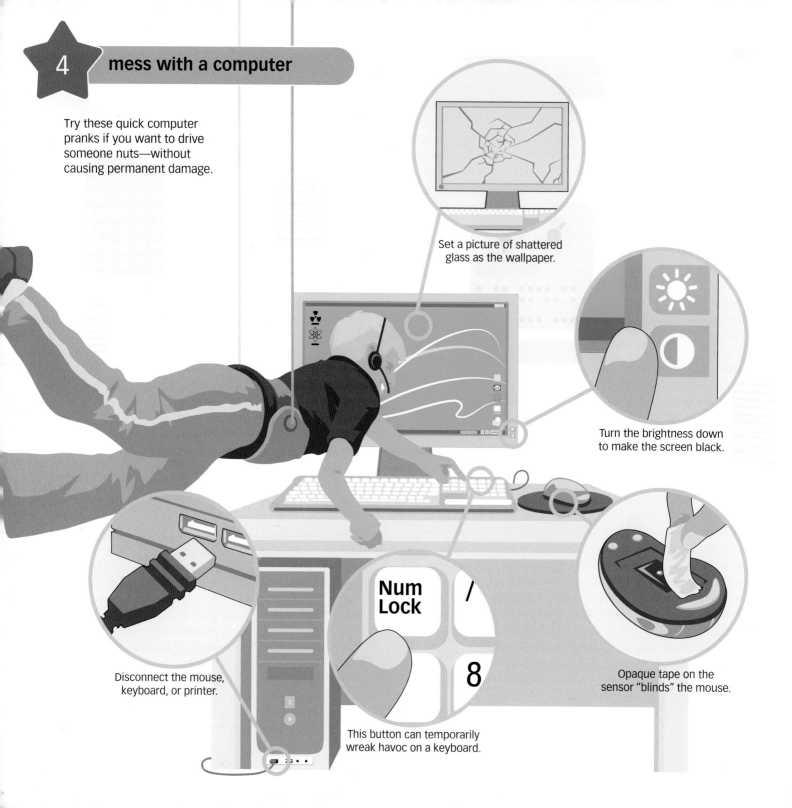

4 mess with a computer

Try these quick computer pranks if you want to drive someone nuts—without causing permanent damage.

Set a picture of shattered glass as the wallpaper.

Turn the brightness down to make the screen black.

Disconnect the mouse, keyboard, or printer.

Num Lock

/

8

This button can temporarily wreak havoc on a keyboard.

Opaque tape on the sensor "blinds" the mouse.

blurry-background action shot

Snap a pic while rotating to follow a moving object.

ant's-eye view

Take a picture with your camera on the ground.

tiny-friend illusion

Have one person stand back and higher up than another.

form shadow puppets

alligator

bird

snake

boar

elephant

horse

standing dog

camel

llama

rabbit

human

deer

goat

turtle

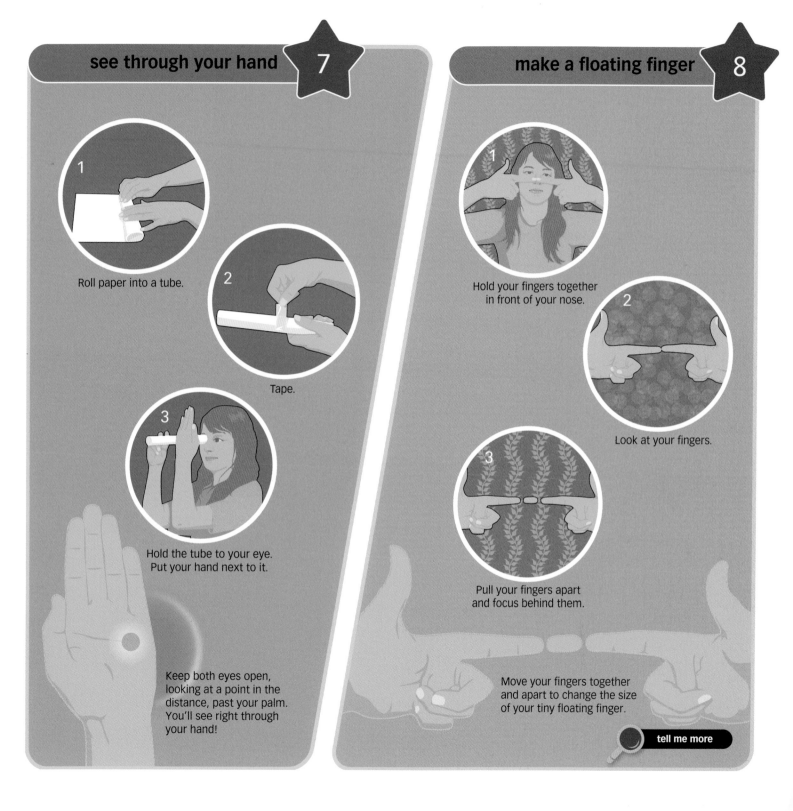

see through your hand ⭐ 7

1. Roll paper into a tube.

2. Tape.

3. Hold the tube to your eye. Put your hand next to it.

Keep both eyes open, looking at a point in the distance, past your palm. You'll see right through your hand!

make a floating finger ⭐ 8

1. Hold your fingers together in front of your nose.

2. Look at your fingers.

3. Pull your fingers apart and focus behind them.

Move your fingers together and apart to change the size of your tiny floating finger.

tell me more

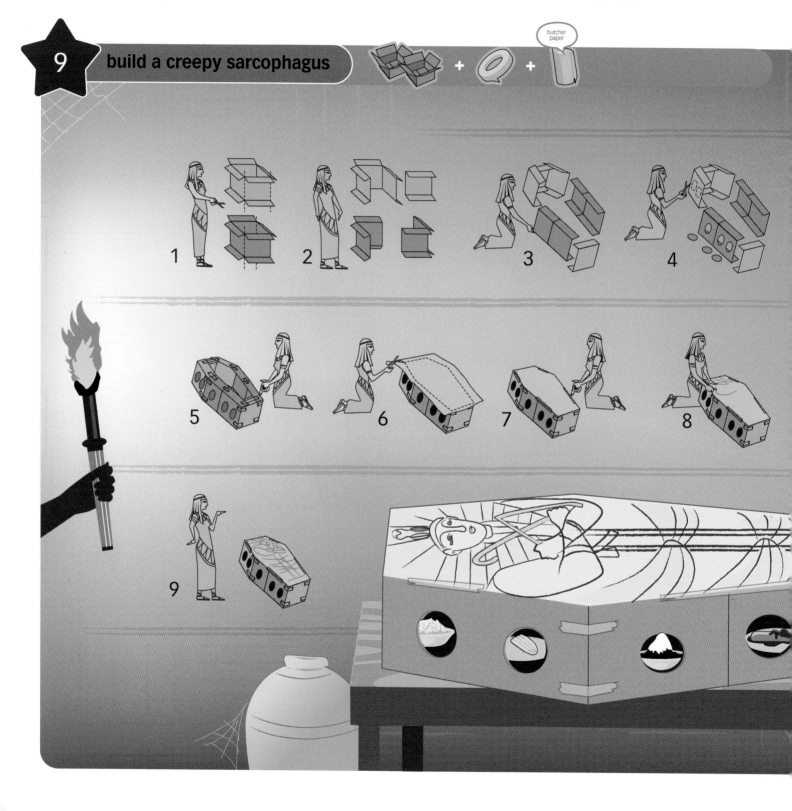

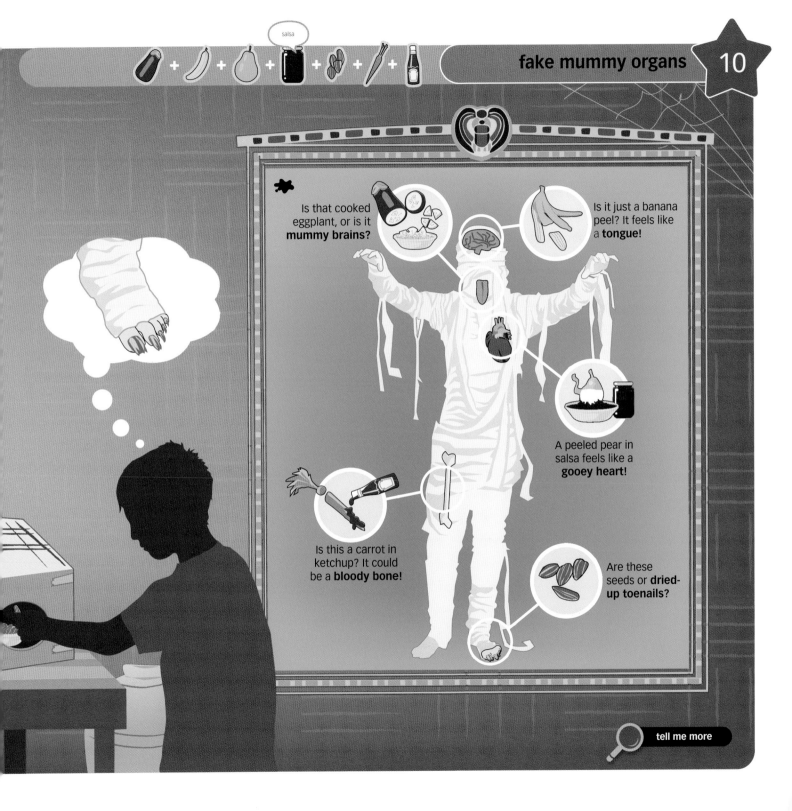

salsa

Is that cooked eggplant, or is it **mummy brains?**

Is it just a banana peel? It feels like a **tongue!**

A peeled pear in salsa feels like a **gooey heart!**

Is this a carrot in ketchup? It could be a **bloody bone!**

Are these seeds or **dried-up toenails?**

tell me more

chicken wire +  + fake fur + felt + + + plastic platter

1

Make a torso with the chicken wire. Stuff it with newspaper, then cover with fake fur.

2

Cut features out of felt and glue on.

3

Decorate overalls to look like chicken legs.

9

Put on the overalls, shirt, and jacket.

Sew the torso to the overalls' back.

8

Cut a slit up a jacket and shirt.

Glue the wings and pants to the platter.

Cut out a space for your hips.

5

Stuff the pants and socks with newspaper. Sew the shoes to the socks, and the socks to the pants.

paint funny feet 12

draw hand costumes 13

create chin people 14

Freak out friends and family alike with a topsy-turvy version of yourself. Turn upside down, and have a friend decorate your chin to look like a face. Weird!

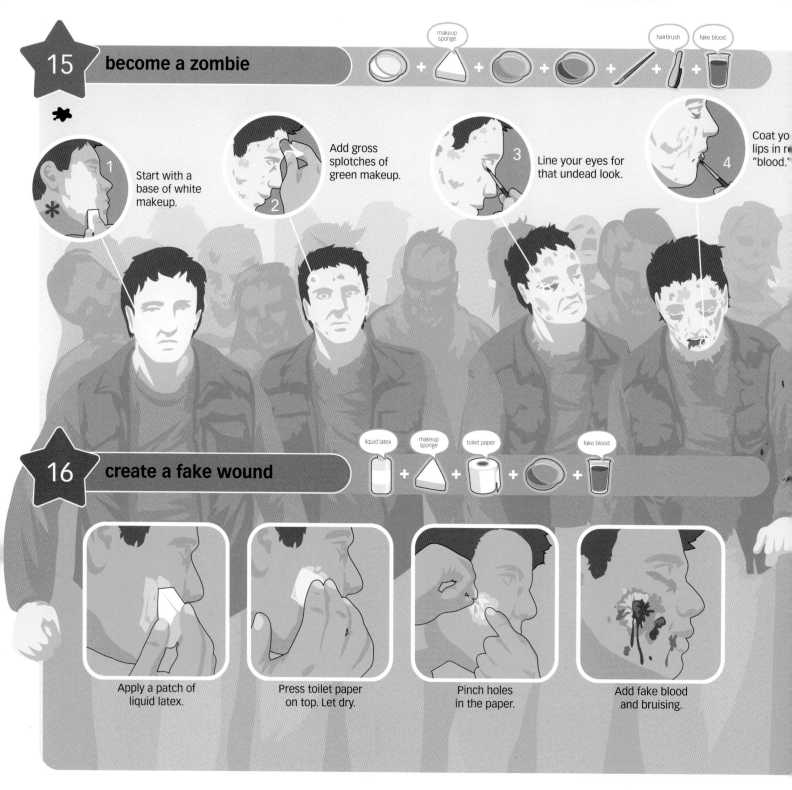

15 become a zombie

makeup sponge · hairbrush · fake blood

1. Start with a base of white makeup.

2. Add gross splotches of green makeup.

3. Line your eyes for that undead look.

4. Coat yo lips in r "blood."

16 create a fake wound

liquid latex · makeup sponge · toilet paper · fake blood

Apply a patch of liquid latex.

Press toilet paper on top. Let dry.

Pinch holes in the paper.

Add fake blood and bruising.

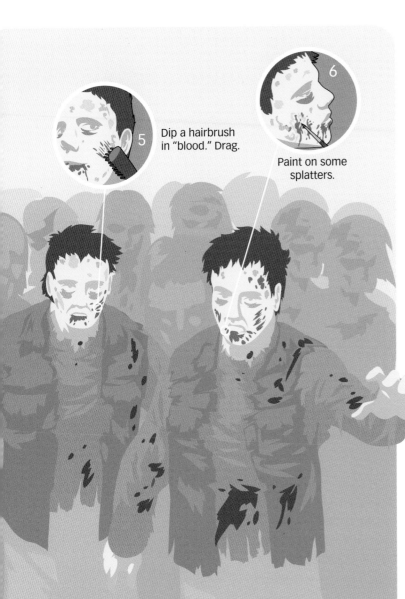

Dip a hairbrush in "blood." Drag.

Paint on some splatters.

Zombies—they're not just for horror movies anymore! The living dead make a festive addition to any school dance, family holiday, or shopping trip. You can pick up the needed makeup at any drugstore or supermarket.

corn syrup + + + paraffin wax +

1 10 drops red food coloring | 1 drop green food coloring

1 c (240 ml) corn syrup

Combine.

2 10 sec — Soften a lump of paraffin wax.

3 Pinch off a piece. Hollow out the inside.

4 Fill with fake blood.

5 Pinch the capsule closed.

6 make edible fake barf 185 — Bite down to spurt the "blood."

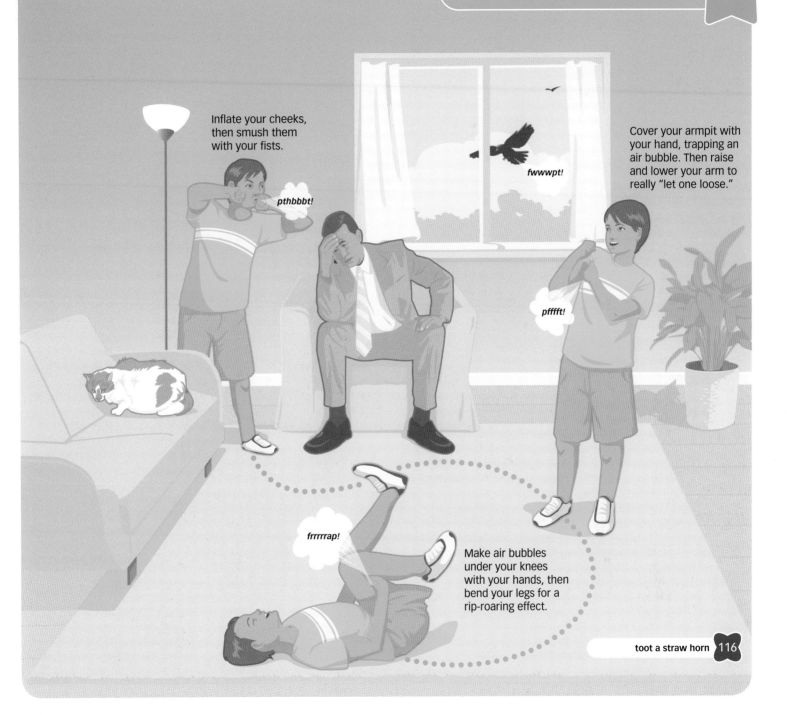

Inflate your cheeks, then smush them with your fists.

pthbbbt!

fwwwpt!

Cover your armpit with your hand, trapping an air bubble. Then raise and lower your arm to really "let one loose."

pfffft!

frrrrrap!

Make air bubbles under your knees with your hands, then bend your legs for a rip-roaring effect.

23 | make a coin jump

Put a coin on each palm, with one near your thumb.

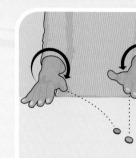

Flip your hands, shooting the coins under one hand.

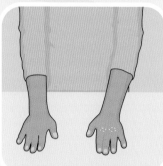

The audience imagines there's a coin under each.

Turn the empty palm. Then reveal the missing coin!

24 | bring a dove back to life

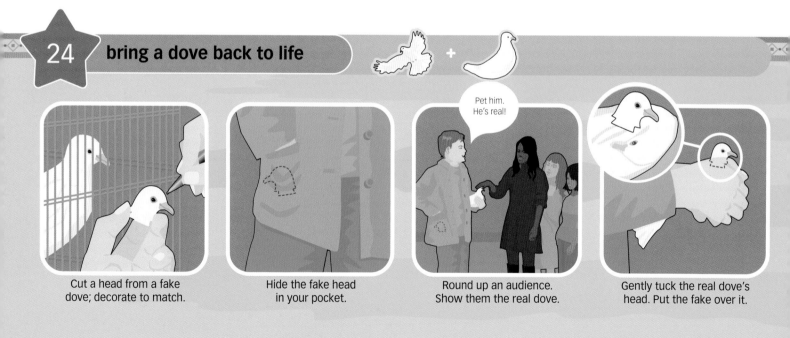

Cut a head from a fake dove; decorate to match.

Hide the fake head in your pocket.

Pet him. He's real!

Round up an audience. Show them the real dove.

Gently tuck the real dove's head. Put the fake over it.

Hang a string over
your palm.

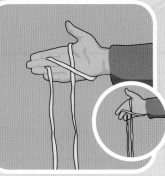

Loop the back end over
your middle finger.

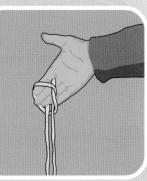

Slide the loop down
around your knuckles.

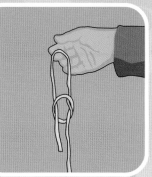

Pull the string between
your fingers up.

149 hollow out a birdhouse

Pull the fake head
away suddenly.

Cover the real dove
with the fake head.

Tuck the fake; blow on the
dove to raise his head.

Release, putting the fake
head back in your pocket.

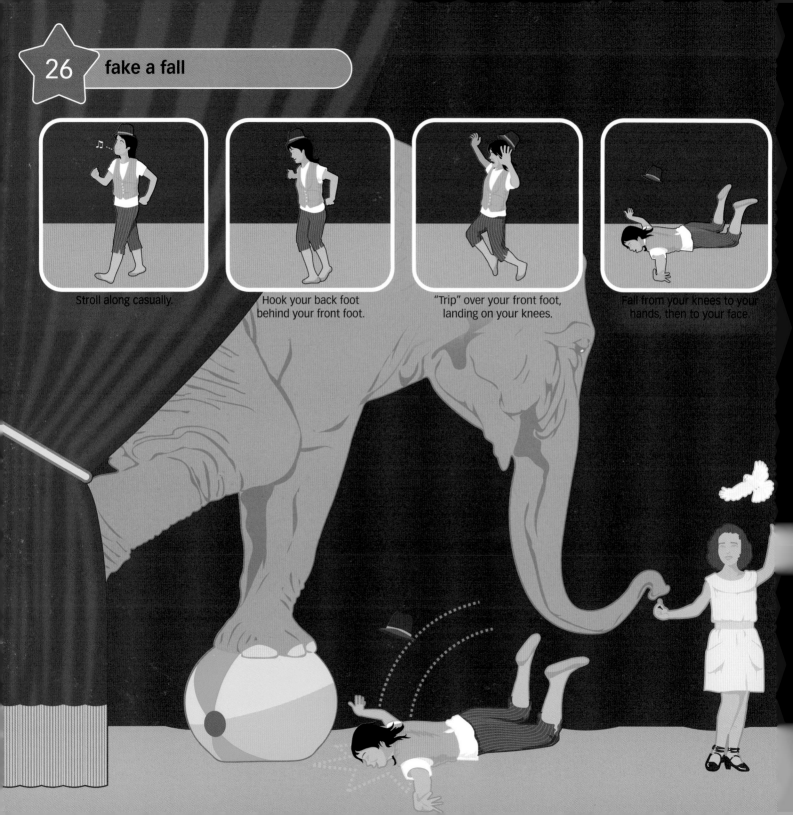

26 fake a fall

Stroll along casually.

Hook your back foot behind your front foot.

"Trip" over your front foot, landing on your knees.

Fall from your knees to your hands, then to your face.

Line up a hat brim with your outstretched arm.

Flick your wrist to roll it quickly down your arm.

Dip your arm to keep up the momentum.

Catch the hat once it reaches your hand.

spin a plate ★28

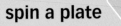
Put a stick under a plastic plate's rim.

Start rotating the stick, holding the bottom still.

When the plate is spinning fast, hold the stick still.

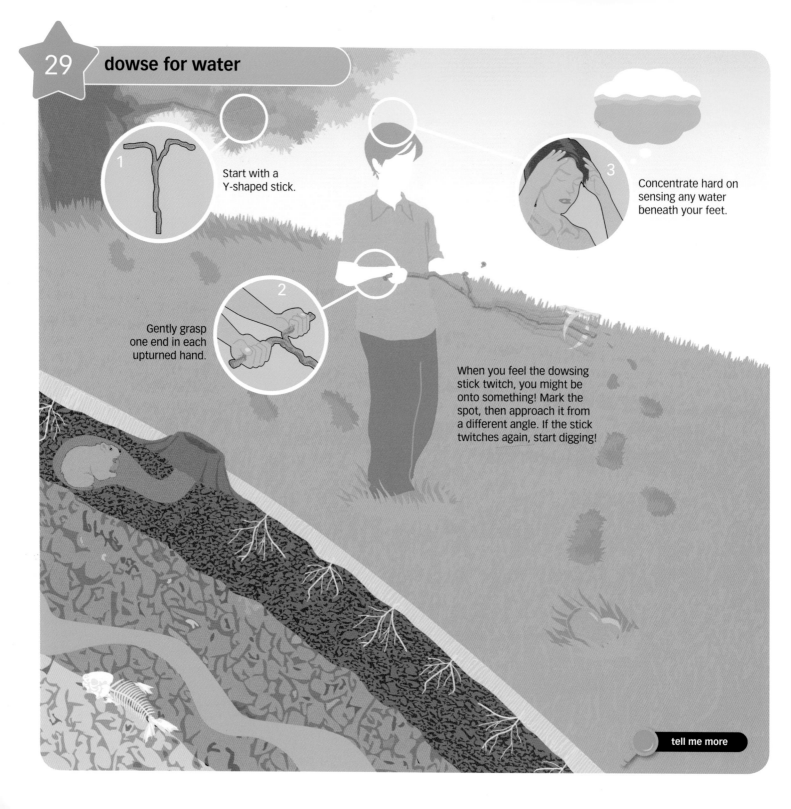

1 Start with a Y-shaped stick.

2 Gently grasp one end in each upturned hand.

3 Concentrate hard on sensing any water beneath your feet.

When you feel the dowsing stick twitch, you might be onto something! Mark the spot, then approach it from a different angle. If the stick twitches again, start digging!

tell me more

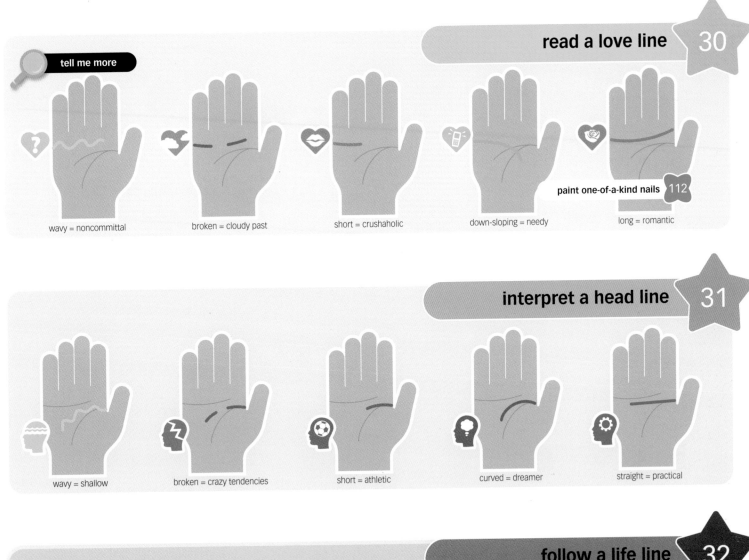

tell me more

wavy = noncommittal

broken = cloudy past

short = crushaholic

down-sloping = needy

long = romantic

paint one-of-a-kind nails 112

wavy = shallow

broken = crazy tendencies

short = athletic

curved = dreamer

straight = practical

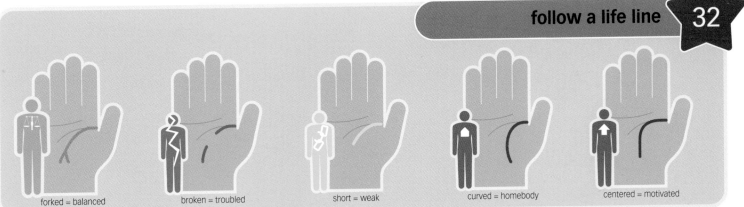

forked = balanced

broken = troubled

short = weak

curved = homebody

centered = motivated

slice an unpeeled banana

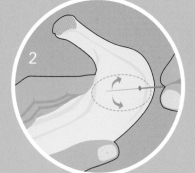

Slide the pin in a circle
inside the peel.

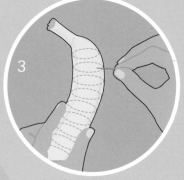

Continue slicing all the
way down the fruit.

Poke a pin into a banana
along one seam.

Hand it to someone who
needs a surprise!

Set the microwave on high for twenty seconds.

:20

1 in (2½ cm)

Arm each marshmallow by inserting a toothpick "spear." When the dust clears and the morphing, oozing, and melting stops, the marshmallow in better shape is the winner.

sculpt snack art 179

tell me more

Chew gum until it's soft.

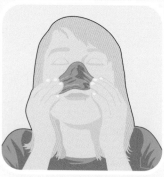

Stretch out the gum. Press to make an airtight seal.

Blow through your nose, holding the gum's edges.

A good bubble-blower "nose" when to stop!

* If you prefer to keep your gum in your mouth, try blowing a bubble inside a bubble! Blow a big bubble, seal it shut, and use the excess gum to blow a small bubble inside it.

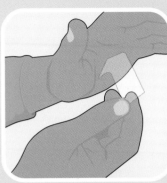

Stick one edge of a piece of tape to your palm.

See? Nothing fishy here . . .

Hand the balloon to a friend for inspection.

Have him inflate it, tie it, and hand it back to you.

Attach the tape in a stealthy manner.

Whoa, dude!

Press the pin into the tape—nothing happens!

Pop the balloon for a big finish.

1

Hook the loop onto
your middle finger.

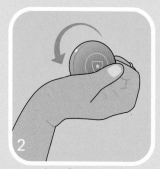

2

Make a fist. Snap your
wrist down hard.

3

Gently lower
the yo-yo.

4

Stop it at the floor.

102 **sketch a dog**

5

The yo-yo will "walk"
on its own.

6

Jerk it back up to
your hand.

38 rock the baby

1

Toss the yo-yo over
the back of your hand.

2

Lift your bottom hand
to double the string.

3

Hook the string with
your thumb.

4

Turn your top hand over
so that it's palm up.

5

Lift your bottom hand.
Pinch the string.

6

Let the baby "rock" in
the string triangle.

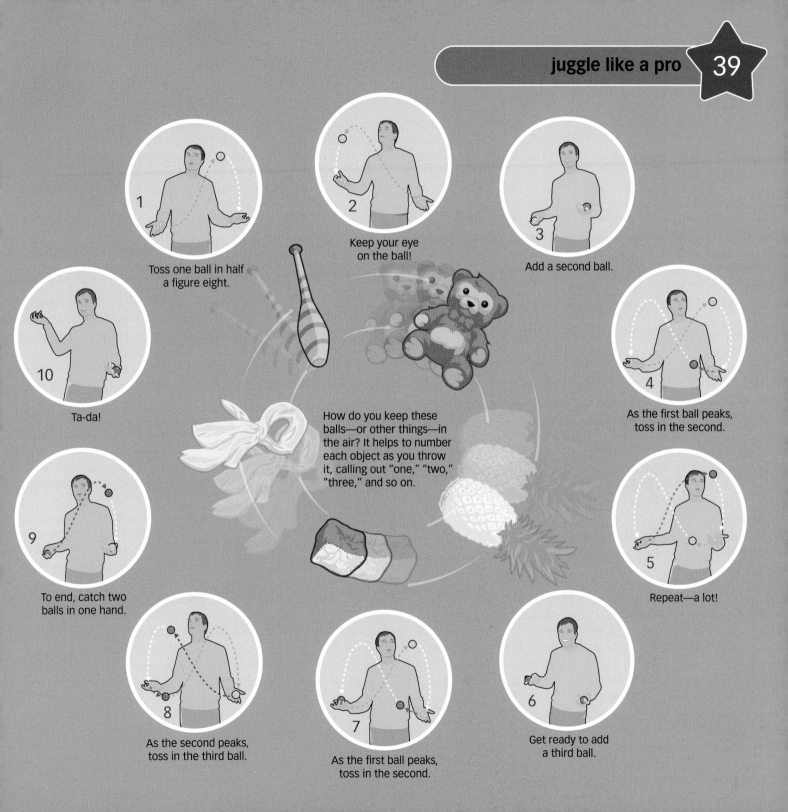

1 Toss one ball in half a figure eight.

2 Keep your eye on the ball!

3 Add a second ball.

4 As the first ball peaks, toss in the second.

5 Repeat—a lot!

6 Get ready to add a third ball.

7 As the first ball peaks, toss in the second.

8 As the second peaks, toss in the third ball.

9 To end, catch two balls in one hand.

10 Ta-da!

How do you keep these balls—or other things—in the air? It helps to number each object as you throw it, calling out "one," "two," "three," and so on.

40 spin a basketball

Hold the ball with just your fingertips.

Spin it up onto one fingertip.

Balance it on your finger until it slows down.

204 sink a free throw

Switch to your other hand. Brush to keep it spinning.

41 skip a stone

Pick a flat, smooth, rounded rock.

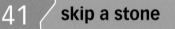

Curl your index finger around it.

Aim to skim the stone along the surface.

Crouch slightly, curling your arm to your body.

Space your feet widely.
Hold the ball palm-down.

Bounce the ball between
your legs. Catch.

Repeat, bouncing
from back to front.

Catch it.

Fling your arm out and
flick your wrist to release.

Watch it skip into
the sunset.

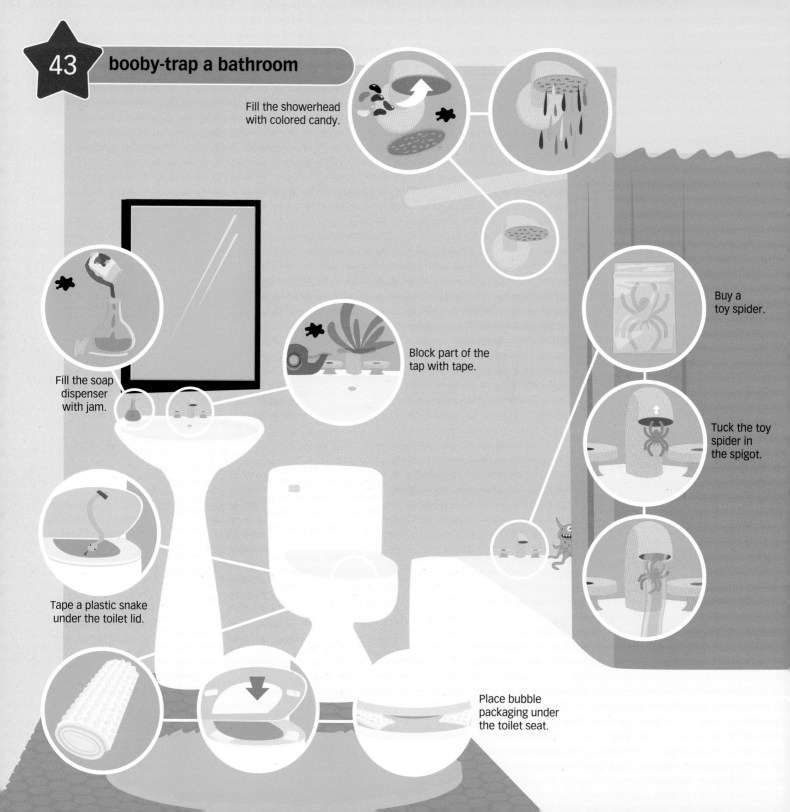

booby-trap a bathroom

Fill the showerhead with colored candy.

Buy a toy spider.

Block part of the tap with tape.

Tuck the toy spider in the spigot.

Fill the soap dispenser with jam.

Tape a plastic snake under the toilet lid.

Place bubble packaging under the toilet seat.

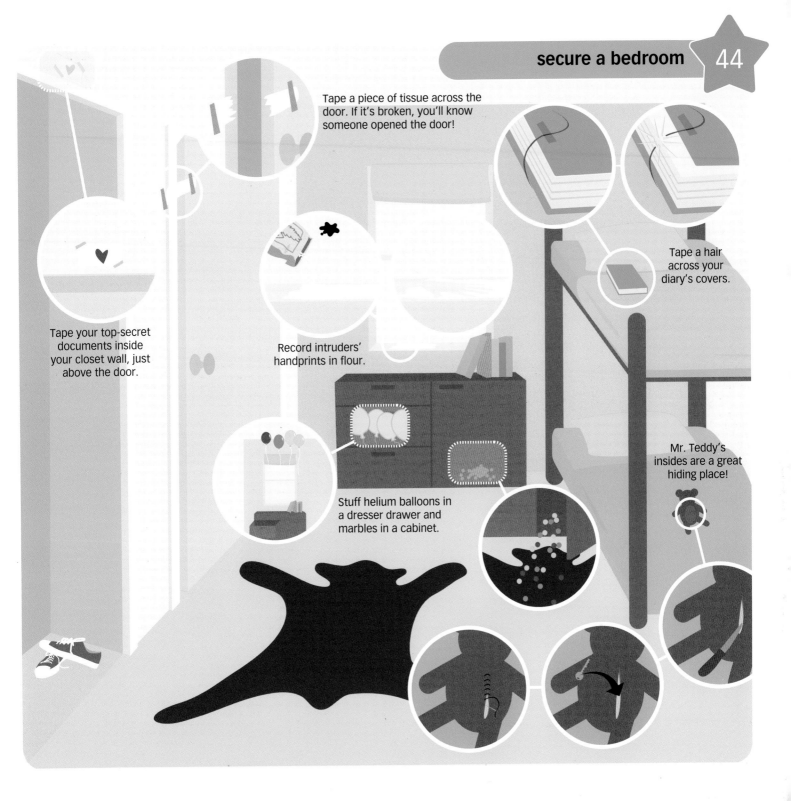

Tape a piece of tissue across the door. If it's broken, you'll know someone opened the door!

Tape a hair across your diary's covers.

Tape your top-secret documents inside your closet wall, just above the door.

Record intruders' handprints in flour.

Mr. Teddy's insides are a great hiding place!

Stuff helium balloons in a dresser drawer and marbles in a cabinet.

45 turn drink mix into hair dye

conditioner + petroleum jelly + + + plastic wrap

1 Apply petroleum jelly around your hairline.

2 Make a paste from drink mix and conditioner.

1 tbsp conditioner

2 packets colored drink mix

3 Work into hair with gloved hands and a toothbrush.

56 light a room with a ponytail

4 Let sit under plastic.

1½ hr

5 Rinse.

This dye job will be subtle and should only last a few washes—unless you have blond hair. Color will be brighter and last *much* longer in light hair.

46 make a "platinum" grill

spirit gum

2 Apply spirit gum to the tooth.

Spirit gum is an adhesive used by theater and movie makeup artists. You can pick some up at a drugstore.

1 Cut out a tooth-size square of foil.

3 Press the foil on. Smooth out any bubbles.

wire clippers needle-nose pliers

Snip the arm of a
safety pin in half.

Put glue on the tip.
Secure the loose end.

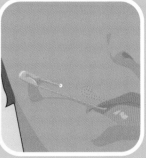

Bend back the very
tip of the pin arm.

Now it's safe to stick
the pin in your cheek.

sport spiky hair 48

hair gel   hair spray

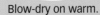

1 Put gel in wet hair.
Twist into spikes.

2 Blow-dry on warm.

3 Set with hair spray.

49   twirl a drumstick

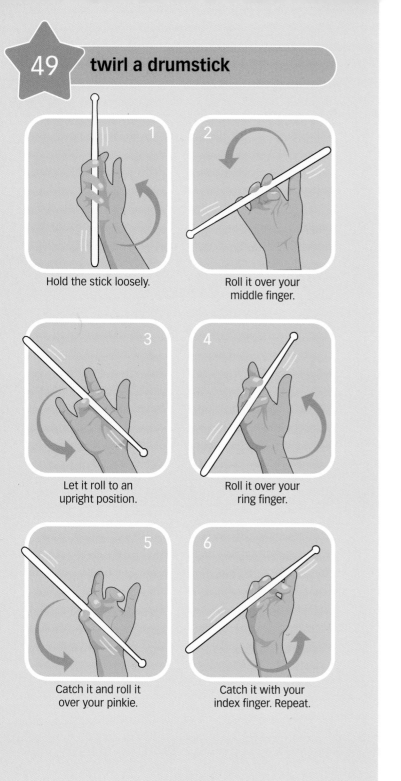

1. Hold the stick loosely.
2. Roll it over your middle finger.
3. Let it roll to an upright position.
4. Roll it over your ring finger.
5. Catch it and roll it over your pinkie.
6. Catch it with your index finger. Repeat.

1. Crouch down low, then spring up.

do a rock-star jump 50

2

Leap up and kick one leg out.

3

Land. Resume rocking.

master the angus spin 51

To get spinning, "walk" your legs so that you make a complete circle.

tell me more

investigate

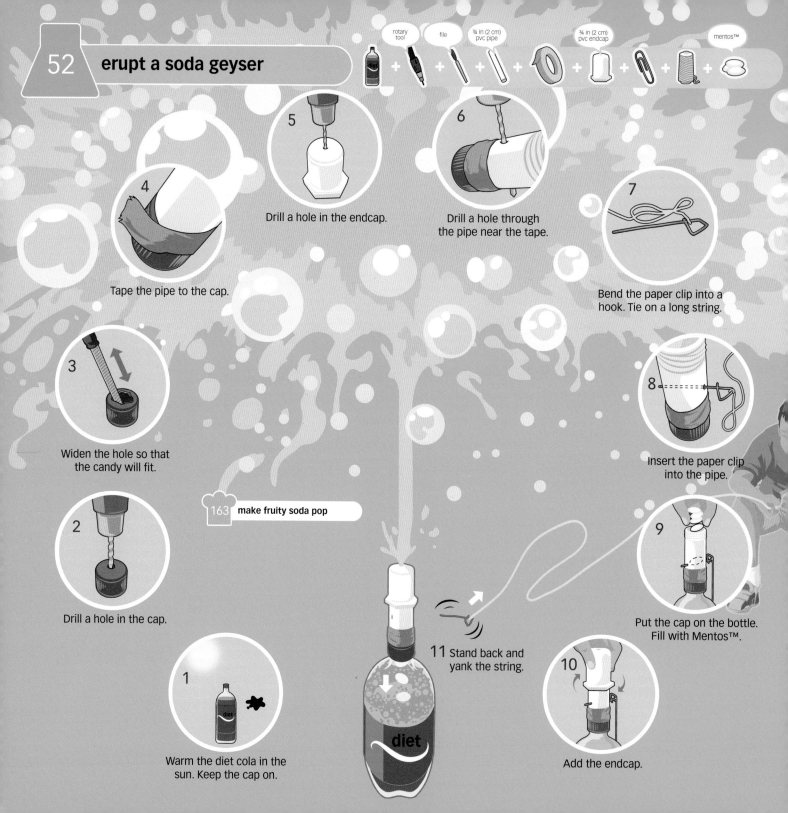

rotary tool + file + ¾ in (2 cm) pvc pipe + ¾ in (2 cm) pvc endcap + mentos™

4 Tape the pipe to the cap.

5 Drill a hole in the endcap.

6 Drill a hole through the pipe near the tape.

7 Bend the paper clip into a hook. Tie on a long string.

3 Widen the hole so that the candy will fit.

163 make fruity soda pop

8 Insert the paper clip into the pipe.

2 Drill a hole in the cap.

9 Put the cap on the bottle. Fill with Mentos™.

1 Warm the diet cola in the sun. Keep the cap on.

11 Stand back and yank the string.

10 Add the endcap.

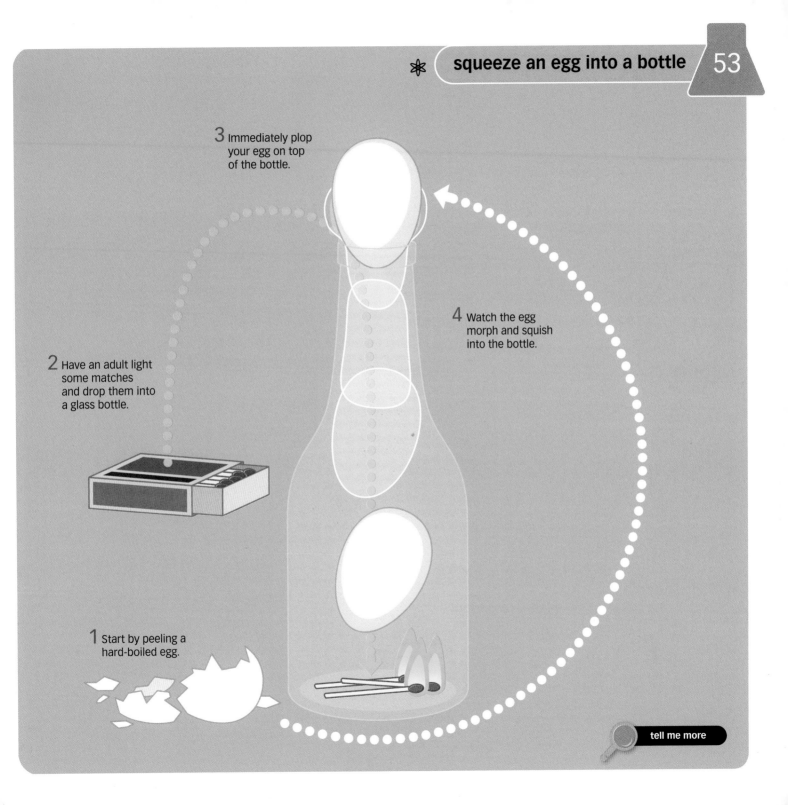

3 Immediately plop your egg on top of the bottle.

4 Watch the egg morph and squish into the bottle.

2 Have an adult light some matches and drop them into a glass bottle.

1 Start by peeling a hard-boiled egg.

tell me more

54 bend water with static

✳

1 Give your hair a good combing.

2 Hold the comb near a running faucet. Watch the water warp!

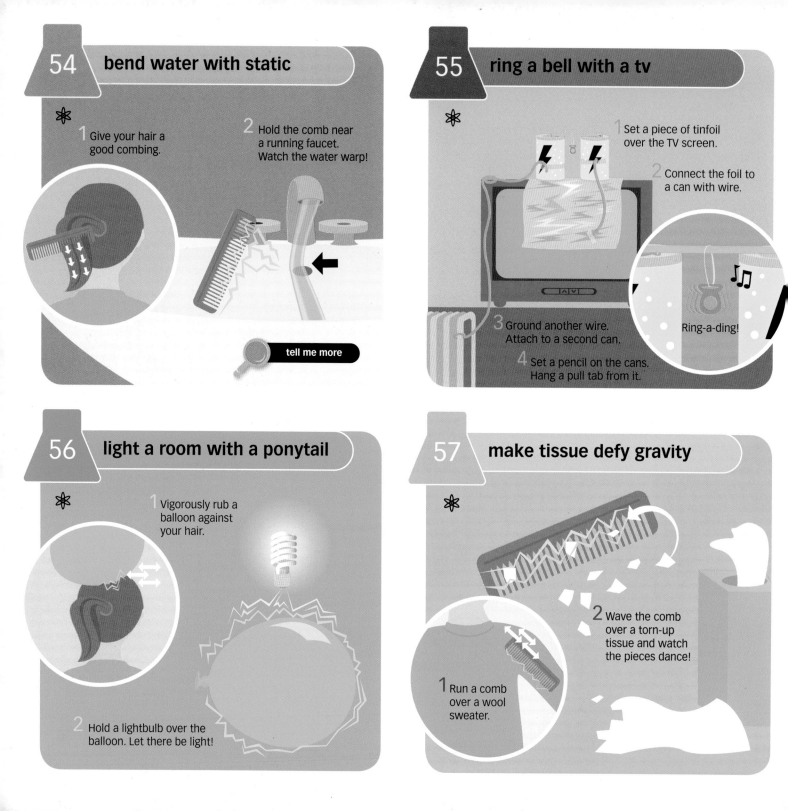

tell me more

55 ring a bell with a tv

✳

1 Set a piece of tinfoil over the TV screen.

2 Connect the foil to a can with wire.

3 Ground another wire. Attach to a second can.

4 Set a pencil on the cans. Hang a pull tab from it.

Ring-a-ding!

56 light a room with a ponytail

✳

1 Vigorously rub a balloon against your hair.

2 Hold a lightbulb over the balloon. Let there be light!

57 make tissue defy gravity

✳

2 Wave the comb over a torn-up tissue and watch the pieces dance!

1 Run a comb over a wool sweater.

Label your taters.

Press a galvanized nail into each potato.

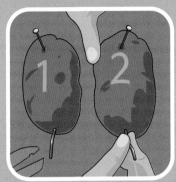

Stick a copper wire into the other end of each.

Remove the digital clock's battery and battery cover.

Connect potato 1's wire to the positive side.

Link 2's nail to the negative side.

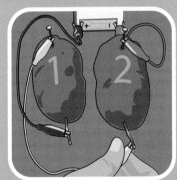

Connect 1's nail to 2's copper wire.

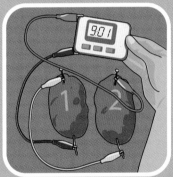

Set your clock to tater-time!

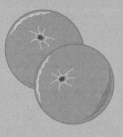

 Potatoes aren't the only powerful food in your kitchen—you can make a food clock out of these ingredients, too.

 tell me more

borax + cornstarch +

½ tsp borax

2 tbsp warm water

Stir to dissolve the borax.

1 tbsp white glue

Pour glue into a jar.

1 tbsp cornstarch

Add cornstarch to the glue.

½ tbsp borax solution

Measure and add the borax solution.

15 sec

Add a few drops of food coloring. Wait.

Stir.

Knead on a clean tabletop.

199   set up a bocce match

Roll into a ball.

* What *is* this magical borax stuff, anyway? It's a mineral used in makeup and soap. It's also used in bug-killer, so store the ball in a plastic bag when you're done, then wash your hands. Whatever you do, don't eat it!

3 tbsp borax

1 c
(240 ml)
very hot
water

Shape a pipe cleaner. Be
sure it will fit into a jar.

Carefully add the
borax to hot water.

4 drops food coloring

Add coloring. Stir until the
borax mostly dissolves.

The pipe cleaner should
hang above the bottom.

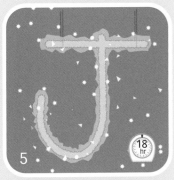

18
hr

Watch your crystals grow.

To display, hang your new
bling with string.

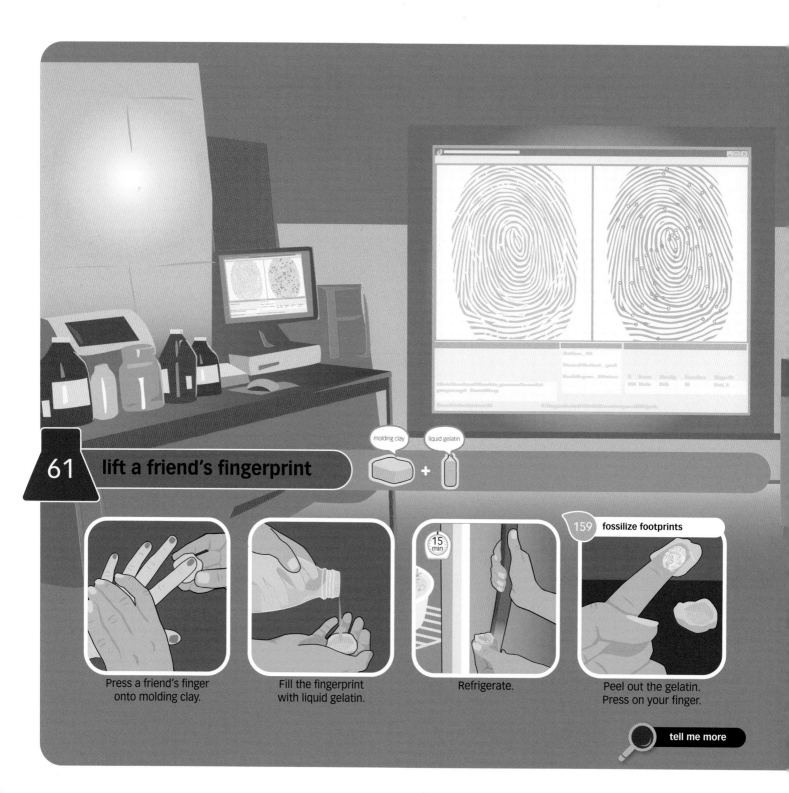

61 lift a friend's fingerprint

molding clay + liquid gelatin

Press a friend's finger onto molding clay.

Fill the fingerprint with liquid gelatin.

15 min

Refrigerate.

159 fossilize footprints

Peel out the gelatin. Press on your finger.

tell me more

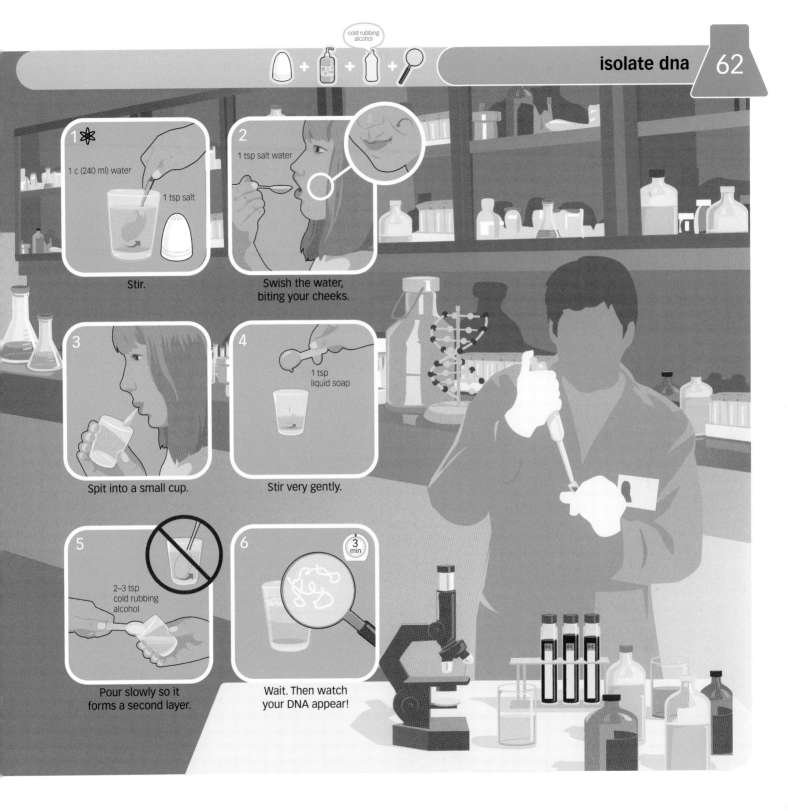

cold rubbing alcohol

1
1 c (240 ml) water
1 tsp salt
Stir.

2
1 tsp salt water
Swish the water, biting your cheeks.

3
Spit into a small cup.

4
1 tsp liquid soap
Stir very gently.

5
2–3 tsp cold rubbing alcohol
Pour slowly so it forms a second layer.

6
3 min
Wait. Then watch your DNA appear!

Cut a narrow paper strip.

Tape and wrap tightly without overlapping.

Tape the other end.

Write lengthwise, one letter per blank space.

Unwrap. It's gibberish! Pass to a trusted pal.

Your friend decodes it with her own pencil.

Change up the objects you wrap the messages around to keep your communications extra safe.

tell me more

m e e t   m e   l 8 r !

★ = quick flash
— = long flash

a ★—	n ★	1 ★————
b —★★★	o ———	2 ★★———
c —★—★	p ★——★	3 ★★★——
d —★★	q ——★—	4 ★★★★—
e ★	r ★—★	5 ★★★★★
f ★★—★	s ★★★	6 —★★★★
g ——★	t —	7 ——★★★
h ★★★★	u ★★—	8 ———★★
i ★★	v ★★★—	9 ————★
j ★———	w ★——	0 —————
k —★—	x —★★—	
l ★—★★	y —★——	
m ——	z ——★★	

If you want to send a secret message across the street, all you need is Morse code and a flashlight. Using the guide at left, write out your message letter by letter, then flash it when the time is right.

Your partner will understand you better if you count to three with your light off between each letter and count to seven with the light off between each word.

tell me more

Are there words or phrases you and your friends say a lot? Make up a shortcut instead of spelling it out. Here are some examples.

★★—★★ "My brother is a dork."
—★—★— "Gotta go—my mom's coming!"
—★—★— "Whatever!"
—★★—★— "You're my BFF."

small mirrors

1

Cut the tops off two cartons.

2

Cut a window near the bottom of one carton.

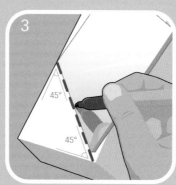

3

Mark a diagonal line as tall as your mirror.

45°
45°

4

Cut on the line; repeat on the carton's opposite side.

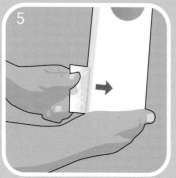

5

Slide a mirror into the slot. Secure with tape.

6

Look in the window—you should see the ceiling.

7

Repeat the process on the second carton.

11

Get your spy on!

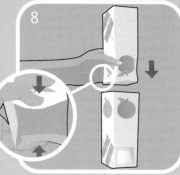

8

Flip one. Insert with the window facing backward.

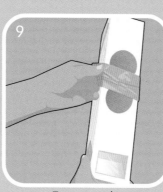

9

Tape securely.

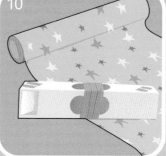

10

Decorate your periscope.

Juice half a lemon.

Paint a message with
the juice. Let it dry.

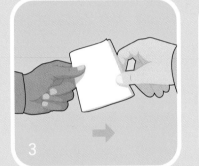

Hand the "blank"
paper to a friend.

Heat reveals your
juicy secret!

If you want to get extra stealthy, wait for the
lemon juice to dry, then write a decoy message
in regular ink on top. When you heat the paper,
the secret message will rise to the top!

tell me more

turn the world upside down

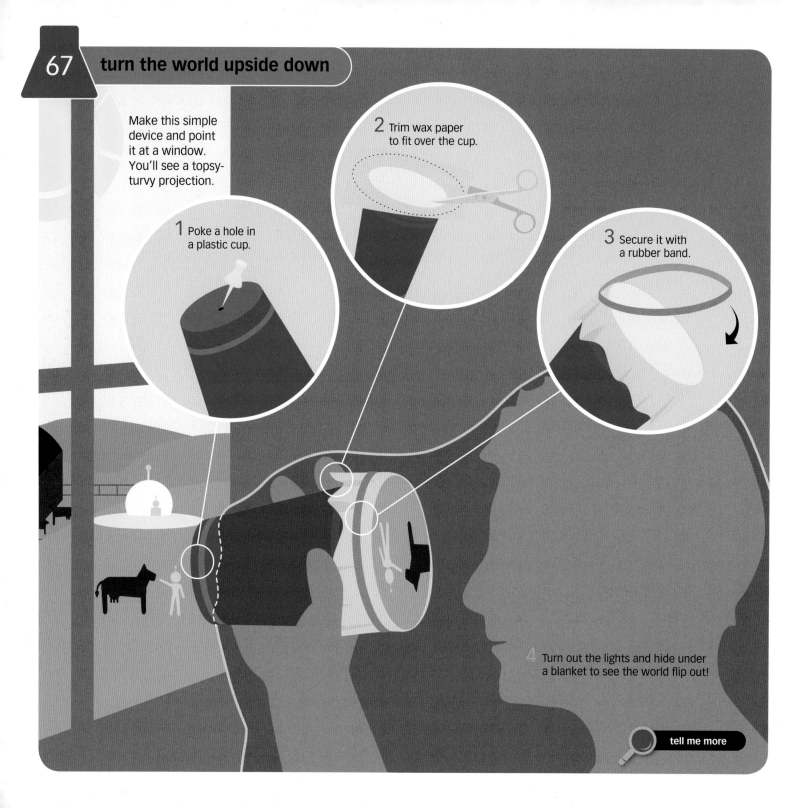

Make this simple device and point it at a window. You'll see a topsy-turvy projection.

1 Poke a hole in a plastic cup.

2 Trim wax paper to fit over the cup.

3 Secure it with a rubber band.

4 Turn out the lights and hide under a blanket to see the world flip out!

tell me more

spin a mini kaleidoscope 68

empty pill bottle + clear plastic lid + old CD + super glue

Saw off a bottle's bottom and its cap's top.

Trace the cap onto a lid three times and cut.

Glue circles to the cap top and the bottle top.

Make a stencil the same length as the bottle. Cut out.

Trace onto the CD. Cut out.

Slide in the CD strips. Trim to fit.

Glue a window to the bottom of the bottle.

Draw a pattern on the cap window.

Decorate the bottle. Put beads in the cap and screw on.

Be careful! If you look straight at an eclipse, you'll injure your eyes. Instead, use a handy eclipse viewer for your own private sun show!

1 Tape a sheet of paper inside a box.

2 Cut an opening opposite the paper.

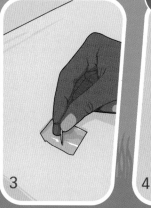

3 Tape tinfoil over the opening. Prick a hole.

124 spot pictures in the moon

4 Cut a space for your head.

Use the longest box you can find to get an extra-large projection.

cyanotype paper

plastic sheet

Gather some
interesting objects.

Arrange the pieces
on cyanotype paper.

Set a clear cover on
top. Leave in the sun.

5–7 min

Remove everything.

Rinse the paper in
a pan of water.

Set on paper to dry. A
sun print appears!

1–2 hr

tell me more

71 get cooking in a solar oven

 black construction paper plastic sheet

Draw a square on a pizza box lid near the edges.

Cut along three of the lines to make a flap.

Open the flap and fold it back.

Wrap and tape tinfoil inside the flap.

72 rig a lightbulb

 insulated copper wire picture-hanging wire 6-volt dry cell battery

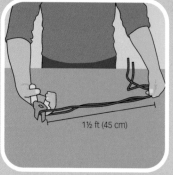

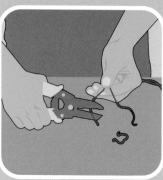

1½ ft (45 cm)

Cut a copper wire in half.

Strip the insulation from the ends.

Poke holes in the lid of a glass jar.

Bend the wires through and shape into hooks.

Line the inside of the
box with tinfoil.

Set a piece of heavy black
paper on the bottom.

Prop the top open so it
gets lots of sunlight.

Add a treat and cover
with clear plastic.

 Once the light burns out, give the wires
plenty of time to cool off before touching!

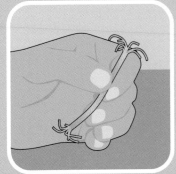

Unravel the ends of
a bit of picture wire.

Twist the wire ends
around the hooks.

Add the jar.

Touch the wires to the
battery terminals.

trap shadows

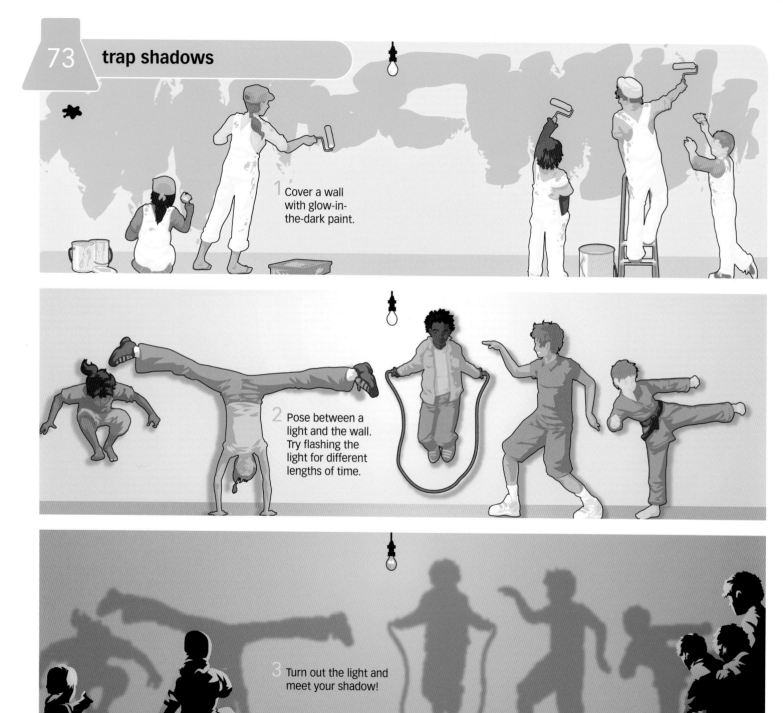

1 Cover a wall with glow-in-the-dark paint.

2 Pose between a light and the wall. Try flashing the light for different lengths of time.

3 Turn out the light and meet your shadow!

5 drops food coloring

6 c (1½ l) water

1

½ c (120 ml) vegetable oil

fill a sea globe 89

2

3

4

Salt is the magic ingredient—your "lava" will keep flowing as long as you continue adding salt. Turn out the lights and hold the bottle over a flashlight to make a lamp that's supergroovy.

2 LED bulbs + watch battery

Remove the matches.

Mark two dots where the lights will go.

Poke two holes.

Insert the LED wires.

Tape both left-hand wires to the matchbook.

Slide the battery under the loose right-hand wires.

Press to test your light.

Tape the edges of the battery to the matchbook.

Shine on!

salsa cup + superglue + double-stick foam tape + vibrating cell-phone motor + watch battery

Glue fringe to a clean salsa cup.

Apply double-stick foam tape to the cup's top.

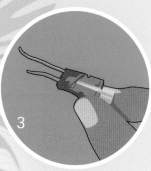

Take the vibrating motor from an old cell phone.

Give your 'bot plenty of room to zip around.

Slip the battery between the wires. It's alive!

Attach the motor. Bend one wire up.

Decorate your 'bot.

vinegar

1. Tape a tin can to a cardboard box top.

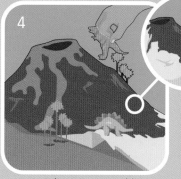

2. Wad up newspaper and tape around the can.

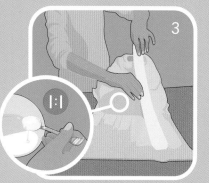

3. Form a volcano with paper dipped in flour and water.

4. Let dry. Decorate with paint and action figures.

5. Fill the can halfway with baking soda.

6. Fill with vinegar dyed with food coloring.

tell me more

Roll an open film canister
or plastic jar in paper.

Tape the tube around
the canister.

Cut out a paper circle and
make a slit to the center.

Fold it into a cone
and tape it on top.

Pour baking soda onto
a square of toilet paper.

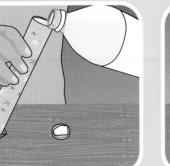

Tape it into a packet and
take everything outdoors.

Set the packet in
the canister lid.

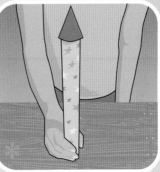

Fill half the canister with
vinegar. Put on the lid.

Flip the rocket over and
stand back for blastoff!

You're building a pretty
powerful rocket here.
Always point it away from
people and windows!

create

32 craft sticks

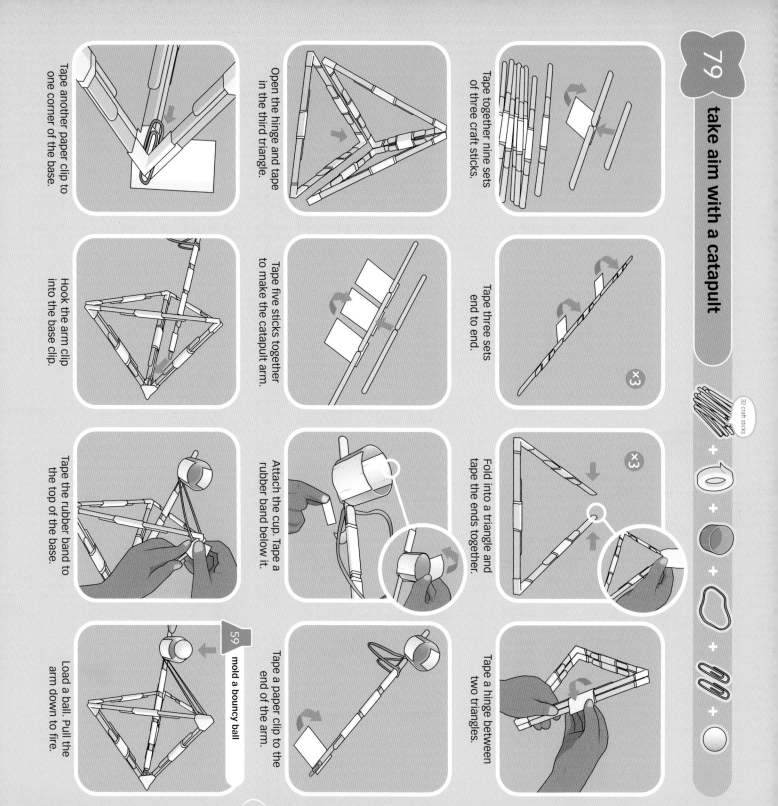

Tape together nine sets of three craft sticks.

Open the hinge and tape in the third triangle.

Tape another paper clip to one corner of the base.

Tape three sets end to end.

×3

Tape five sticks together to make the catapult arm.

Hook the arm clip into the base clip.

Fold into a triangle and tape the ends together.

×3

Attach the cup. Tape a rubber band below it.

Tape the rubber band to the top of the base.

Tape a hinge between two triangles.

Tape a paper clip to the end of the arm.

59 mold a bouncy ball

Load a ball. Pull the arm down to fire.

fire a pen crossbow

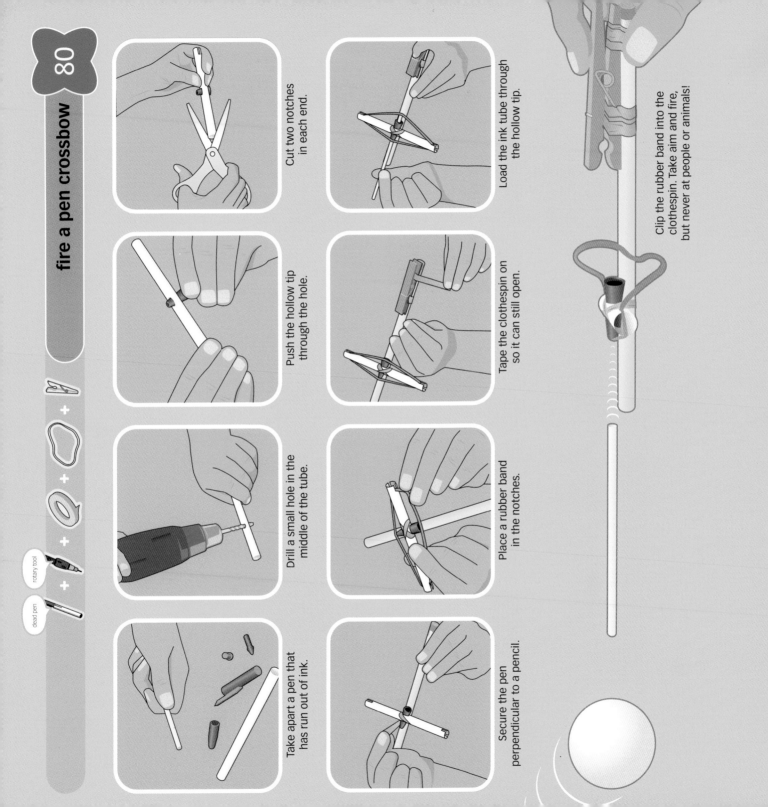

dead pen

rotary tool

Cut two notches in each end.

Push the hollow tip through the hole.

Drill a small hole in the middle of the tube.

Take apart a pen that has run out of ink.

Load the ink tube through the hollow tip.

Tape the clothespin on so it can still open.

Place a rubber band in the notches.

Secure the pen perpendicular to a pencil.

Clip the rubber band into the clothespin. Take aim and fire, but never at people or animals!

You can make a kite with lots of things you find around your house. Decorate a garbage bag or old umbrella fabric for the sail, for instance, and use fabric strips for the tail.

1

40 in (100 cm)

35 in (90 cm)

Make a cross shape with the dowels.

2

Wrap string tightly at the joint. Tie.

3

Notch the ends of the shorter stick.

4

Wrap with string. Make loops at the top and bottom. Tie.

5

1 in (2½ cm)

Trace an outline on the paper.

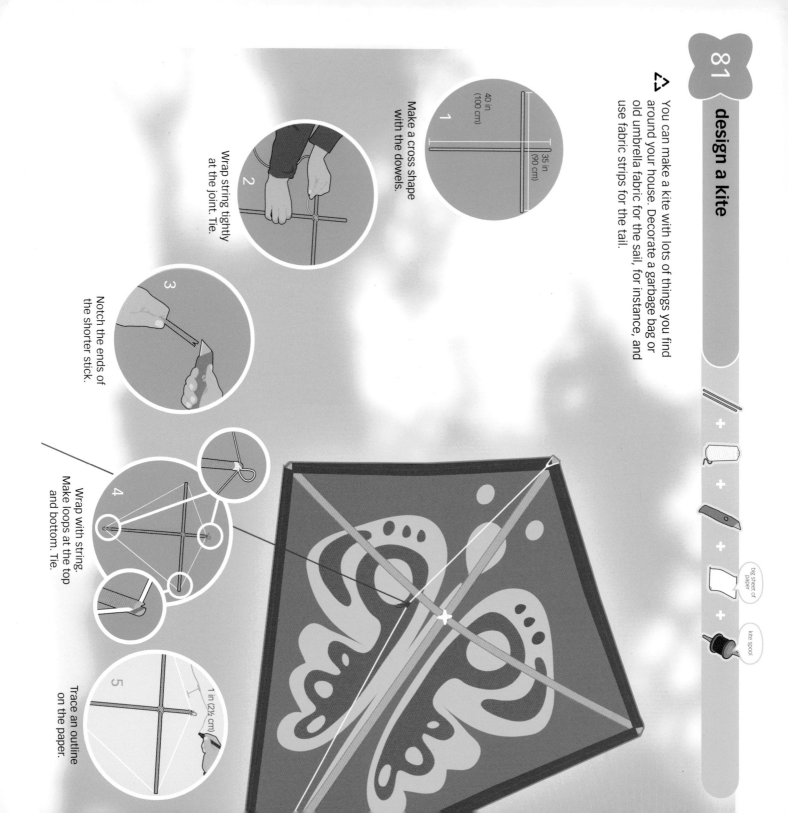

big sheet of paper

kite spool

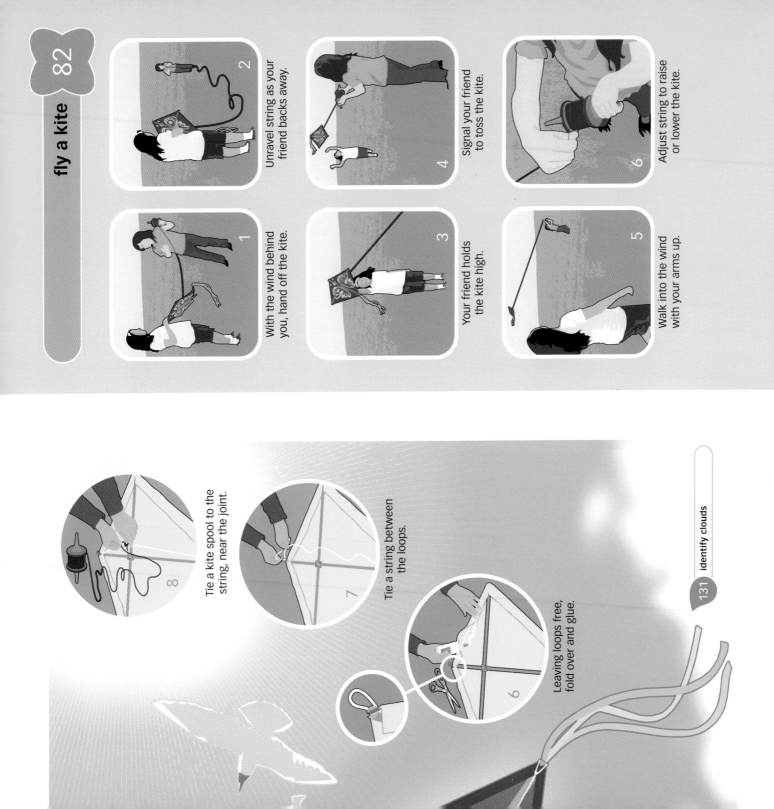

1 With the wind behind you, hand off the kite.

2 Unravel string as your friend backs away.

3 Your friend holds the kite high.

4 Signal your friend to toss the kite.

5 Walk into the wind with your arms up.

6 Adjust string to raise or lower the kite.

8 Tie a kite spool to the string, near the joint.

7 Tie a string between the loops.

6 Leaving loops free, fold over and glue.

131 identify clouds

fold a paper airplane

1

2

3

4 Turn the paper over, then fold down the corners.

5 Fold in half.

6 Turn the paper to the side, then fold down the wings.

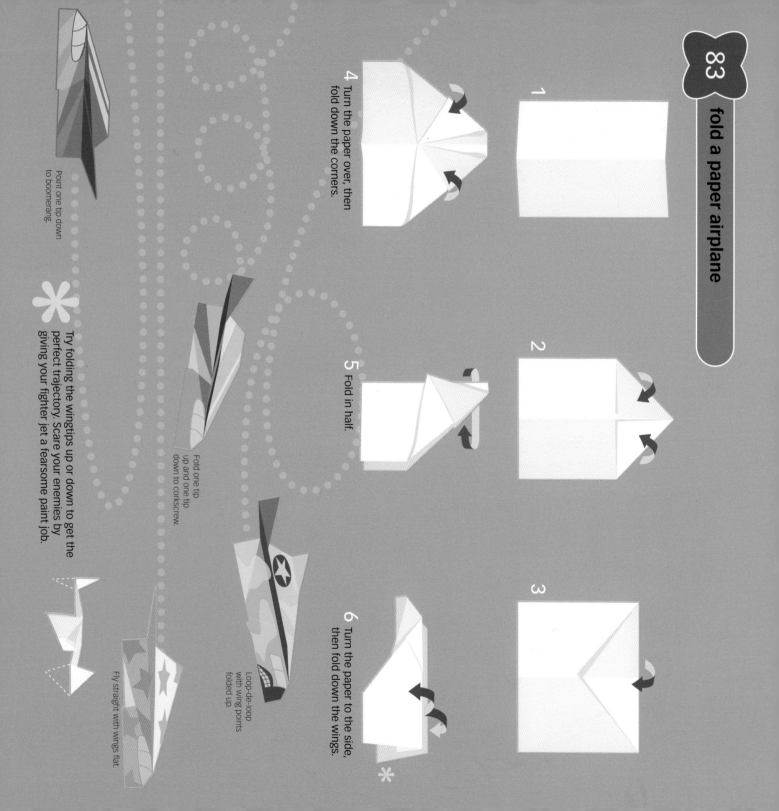

Fold one tip up and one tip down to corkscrew.

Loop-de-loop with wing points folded up.

Point one tip down to boomerang.

Fly straight with wings flat.

* Try folding the wingtips up or down to get the perfect trajectory. Scare your enemies by giving your fighter jet a fearsome paint job.

whip out a ninja star

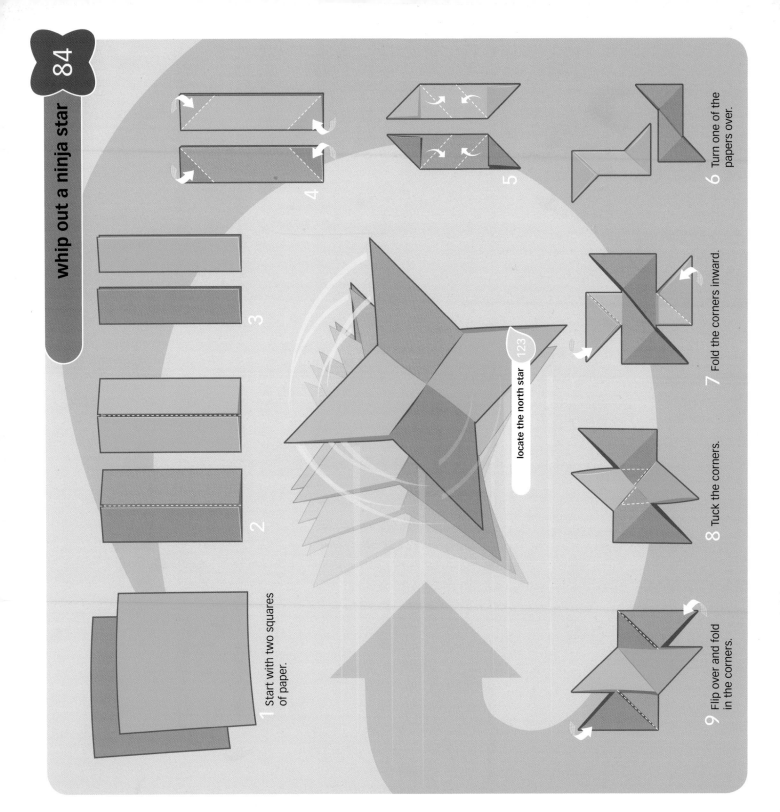

1 Start with two squares of paper.

2

3

4

5

6 Turn one of the papers over.

7 Fold the corners inward.

8 Tuck the corners.

9 Flip over and fold in the corners.

locate the north star 123

liquid starch

+ + ALUM + oil paint +

1

2 c (500 ml)
liquid starch

½ tsp alum

Mix well.

2

**Thin paint with water so it
drips quickly off a spoon.**

3

**Make squiggles and
splotches of paint.**

157 mix up seed paper

4

**Swirl a stick through
the paint.**

5

**Lay a sheet of paper
on the surface.**

6

**Remove the paper and let
the starch water drip off.**

7

**Rinse gently under
cold water.**

tell me more

8

Hang the paper to dry.

9

**Once the paper's dry,
flatten it with a warm iron.**

12 hr

tissue paper

tell me more

Cut along the fold.

Draw a pattern.

Clip the top and bottom.

Fold tissue papers in half, then fold in half again.

Glue a string along the top edge. Fold the edge over.

Unfold and separate.

Cut a pattern along the bottom edges.

Use a hole punch.

light paper-bag luminarias

Fold down the bag's top.

Make patterns with a decorative hole punch. *

craft punch

Cover the bottom with sand.

Set a candle in a small jar.

+ + + + +

---

paste up a piñata

tell me more

Tape newspaper cones to a balloon. ✱

Mix one part water with one part flour. ⚌

Dip newspaper in the mix. Cover the balloon. Let dry. 12 hr

Pop the balloon.

36
stick a pin in a balloon

+ + + + + +

Remove the balloon, then fill the piñata with treats.

Poke a hole near the large opening.

Thread a string through the two holes. Seal.

Decorate your piñata with paint and streamers, then give it a good whack!

Nestle the jar in the sand.

Have an adult light the candle.

Use stencils and a craft knife to make festive designs for any occasion.

1 Clean a small jar and remove the label.

distilled water

2 Soak beach shells and sand to clean.

3 drops mineral oil

distilled water

3

99 mold clay monsters

6

5

4

Fill a pot with damp sand.

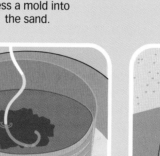
Press a mold into the sand.

Gently remove, pulling straight up.

Press shells into the sides so you see their backs.

Melt candles in a can inside a pan of water.

190°F (90°C)

Dip a string into the wax. Lower the flame.

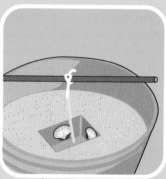
Bury the end of the string in the sand.

Set a stick on top of the pot and tie on the string.

Remove the can.

Carefully fill the hole with hot wax.

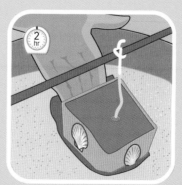
2 hr
Let the wax cool, then remove your candle.

Ask an adult to light the candle.

old candle ends

Tie four threads together. Flatten.

Tape down.

Knot the first thread around the second.

Pull tight, and knot it again.

Knot it around the third thread.

Knot it around the fourth thread.

Start again with the new first thread.

Continue until it fits your wrist. Tie off.

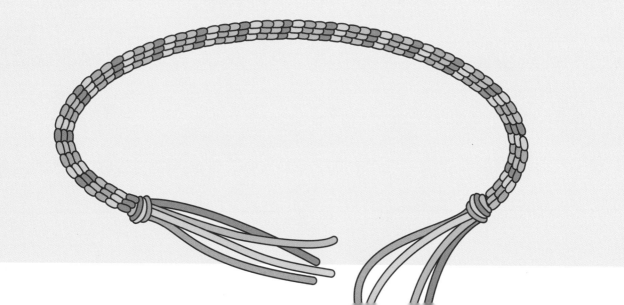

2 ft (60 cm)

blow a nose bubble 35

1

2

3

4

5

6

7

8

9

10

151 dry and press flowers

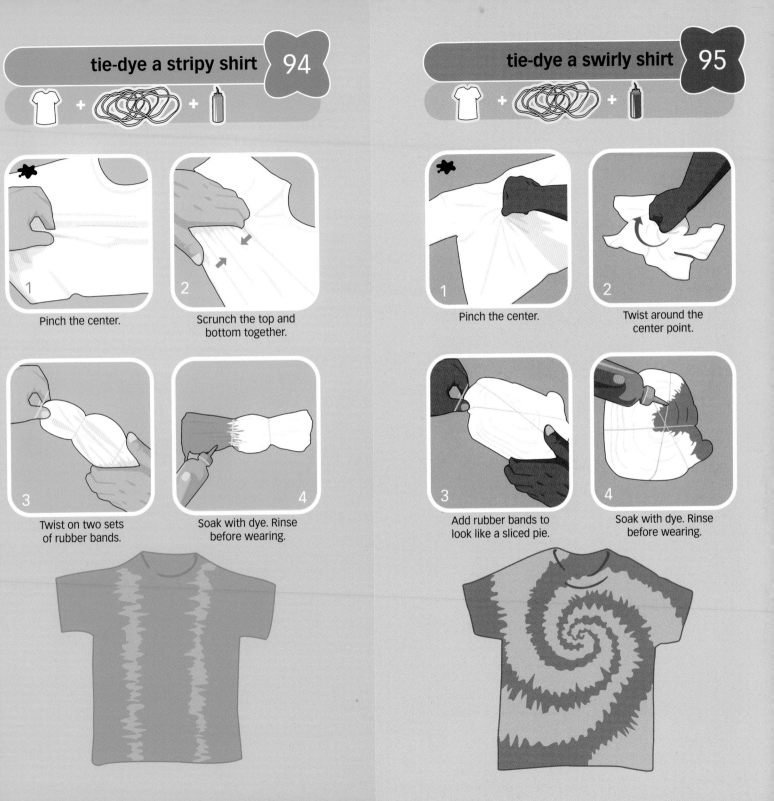

tie-dye a stripy shirt — 94

1. Pinch the center.
2. Scrunch the top and bottom together.
3. Twist on two sets of rubber bands.
4. Soak with dye. Rinse before wearing.

tie-dye a swirly shirt — 95

1. Pinch the center.
2. Twist around the center point.
3. Add rubber bands to look like a sliced pie.
4. Soak with dye. Rinse before wearing.

clear tape

Trace the mp3 player.

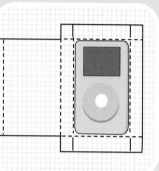

Measure and draw the
sides, back, and tabs.

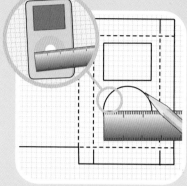

Draw the click wheel,
screen, holes, and buttons.

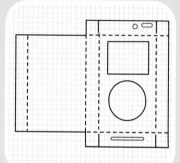

Check that you've drawn
all the tabs and parts.

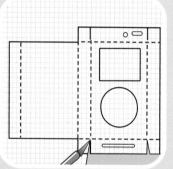

Cut out the template.
Make notches in the tabs.

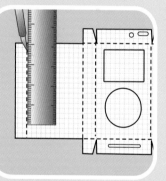

Using the back of an art
knife, score the fold lines.

Test out your template.
Adjust if needed.

Flip it over and cover
one side in duct tape.

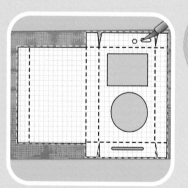

Trim the excess tape.
Cut away all holes.

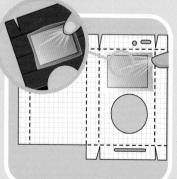

Protect the screen with
clear tape on both sides.

A tiny piece of tape closes
the top for easy access.

Rock on!

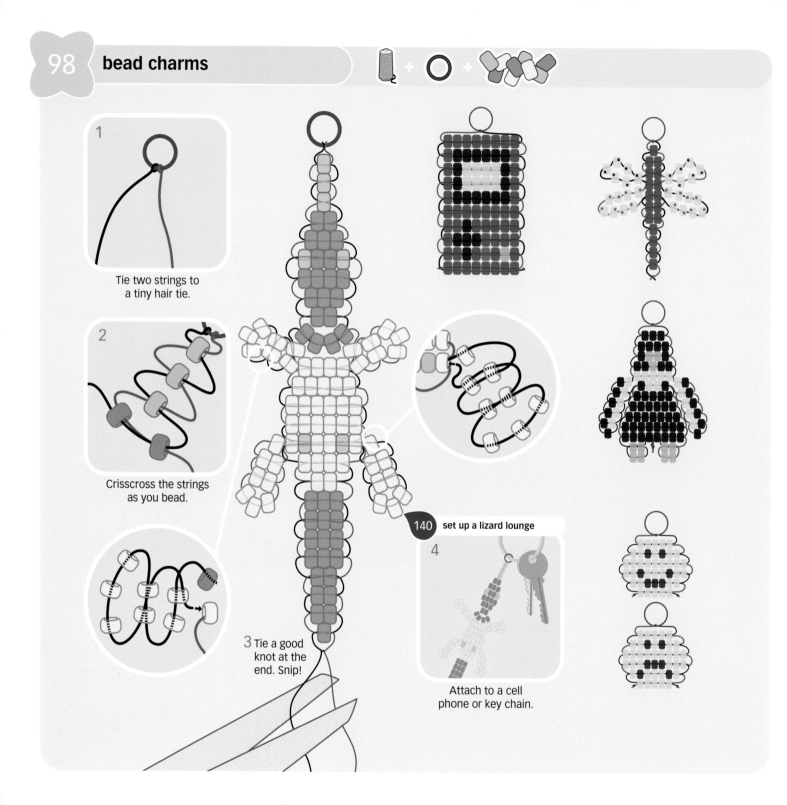

1 Tie two strings to a tiny hair tie.

2 Crisscross the strings as you bead.

3 Tie a good knot at the end. Snip!

140 set up a lizard lounge

4 Attach to a cell phone or key chain.

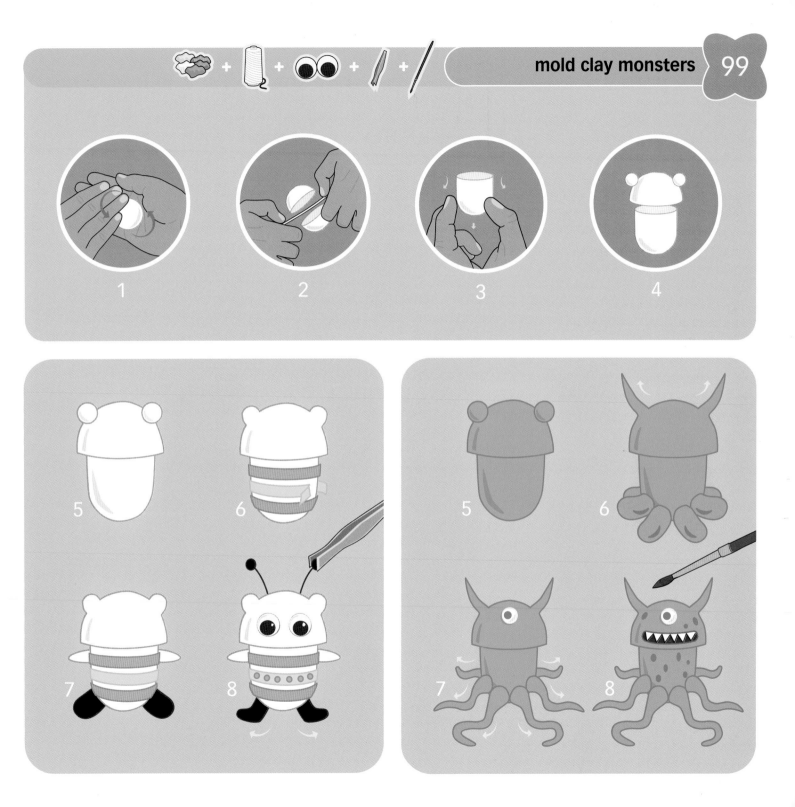

72 rig a lightbulb

draw a cat 101

sketch a dog 102

greet a new dog 136

draft a horse 103

tell me more

105 **flip out with a flip book**

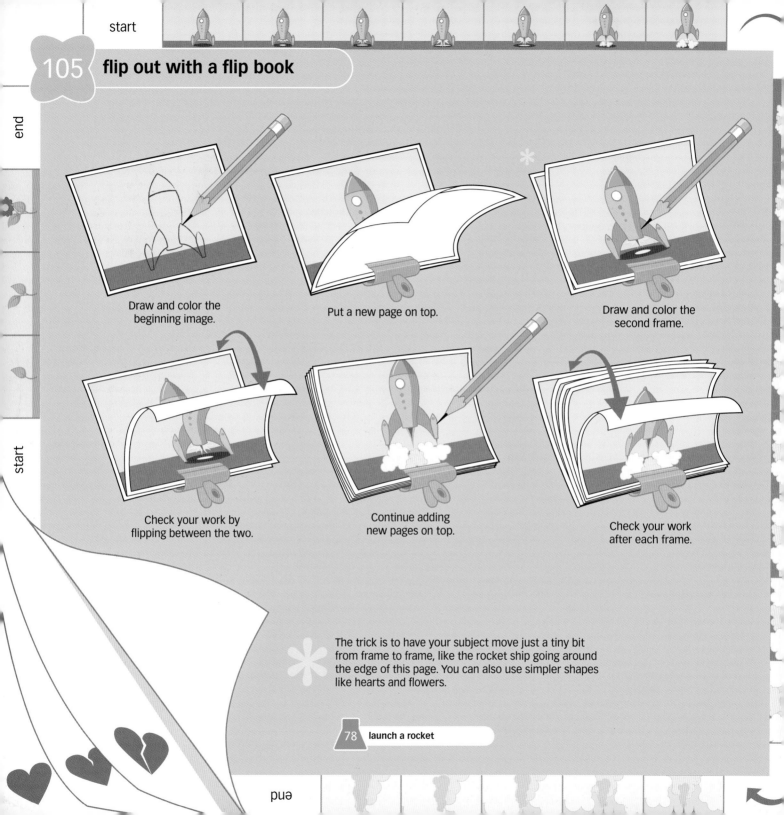

Draw and color the beginning image.

Put a new page on top.

Draw and color the second frame.

Check your work by flipping between the two.

Continue adding new pages on top.

Check your work after each frame.

The trick is to have your subject move just a tiny bit from frame to frame, like the rocket ship going around the edge of this page. You can also use simpler shapes like hearts and flowers.

78 **launch a rocket**

1

2

3 Unfold and push up the "steps."

4

5 Unfold and push up the new "steps."

6

clear contact paper + ruler + comics + tape + fastener

8 in (20 cm)

11 in (28 cm)

3 in (8 cm)

3 in (8 cm)   8 in (20 cm)

1 Draw the template onto clear contact paper.

2 Cut out the template.

3 Arrange the comics on the template. Trim them to fit.

4 Expose the sticky side and place comics facedown.

5 ✱ Cover the other side with contact paper. Trim.

6 Fold tabs up and tape.

3 in (8 cm)

8 in (20 cm)

11 in (28 cm)

3 in (8 cm)

* Once you've laid out your design, remember to stick the comics to the contact paper facedown.

12 Marvel at your new bag!

11 Add a fastener.

7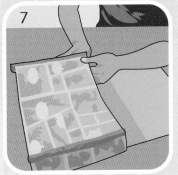

Reinforce all seams, folds, and corners with tape.

8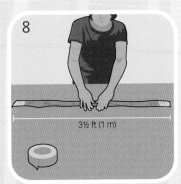

3½ ft (1 m)

Make the strap by sticking two strips together.

9 Set the strap inside the bag and tape.

10 Tape the strap to the outside, too.

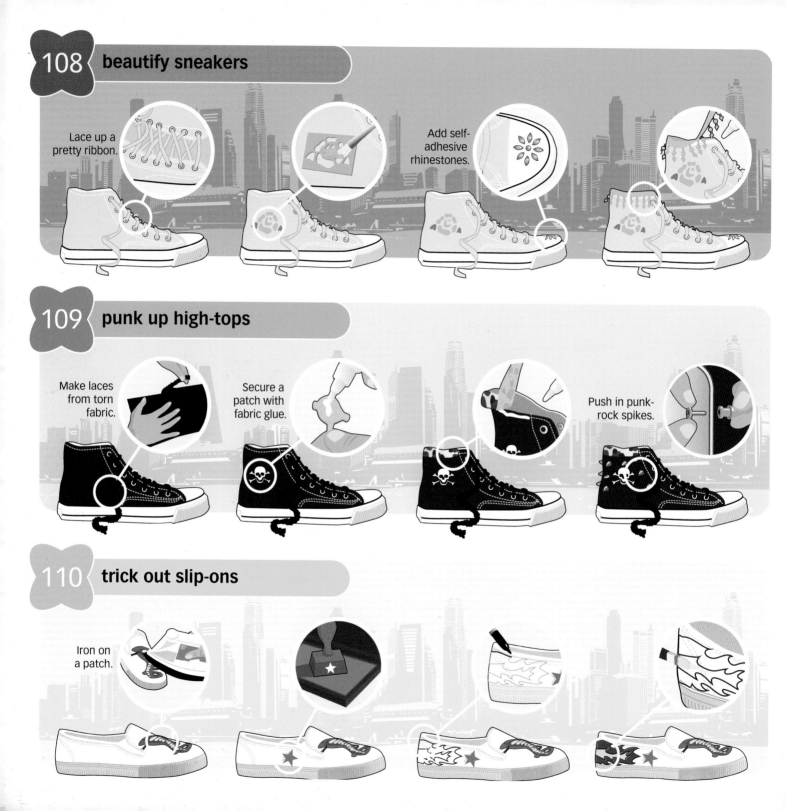

108 beautify sneakers

Lace up a pretty ribbon.

Add self-adhesive rhinestones.

109 punk up high-tops

Make laces from torn fabric.

Secure a patch with fabric glue.

Push in punk-rock spikes.

110 trick out slip-ons

Iron on a patch.

Cut off the legs.

Open up the leg and crotch seams.

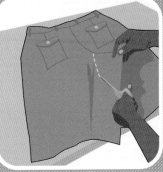

Trim extra fabric from pants' front and back.

Glue down the back flap.

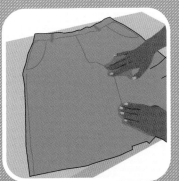

Flip the skirt over and glue down the front flap.

Let the glue dry. Decorate with fabric paint.

1

2
Add to
wet polish.

1
Let dry.

2

1
2

3
Press onto polish.
Let dry.

4

1
Let dry.

2

3

1
Let dry.

2

3

Loop lots of yarn
around your forearm.

Snip.

Separate ten to
fifteen strands.

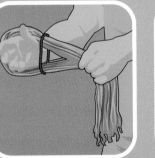

Loop over your wrist.
Slide on a hair tie.

Hold the hair tie. Grab
the yarn near its ends.

Pull yarn through the
loop on your arm.

Ta-da!

Add more yarn
as desired.

Use as a
ponytail holder.

tracing paper + rubbing alcohol +

Apply clear deodorant.

Place the drawing facedown.

Rub with water.

Trace an image.

tell me more

Color with
permanent ink.

Using rubbing alcohol,
blend for a shaded effect.

115   annoy with a balloon horn

film canister

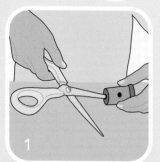

1 Poke a hole in the side and the bottom.

2 Poke a hole in the cap.

3 Slit the balloon in half along its fold.

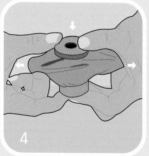

4 Stretch over the bottle. Add the cap.

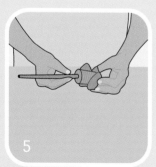

5 Stick the straw into the bottom hole.

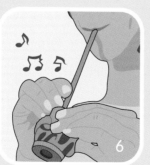

6 Cover part of the side hole and blow.

116   toot a straw horn

1 Cut a straw in half. Discard the bent end.

2 Trim the end as shown.

3 Wrap paper around the straw. Tape.

4 Tape the cone and straw together.

5 Pinch the end of the straw tightly and hold.

45 sec

6 Place between your lips. Honk away!

mini cereal boxes + talking greeting cards + / + old earbuds + electrical tape + ⌨ + 📱

Unfold and flatten the boxes.

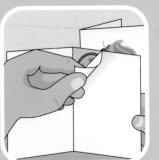
Peel open the greeting cards.

Remove the speaker from each card.

Cut the wires at the circuit board. Strip.

Cut the earbuds off your headphones.

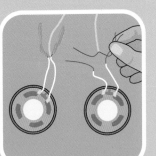
Strip the wires. Cut any fibers from wires.

Twist the wires together and tape.

Trace the speaker on the box and cut out.

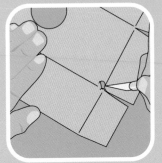
Cut a notch at the bottom for the wires.

Glue each speaker into its window.

Run the wires out the notches. Glue shut.

moonwalk in style 213

Plug in and rock out!

transparency paper + photo emulsion + framed mesh screen + squeegee + glass + + + + +

Design a sweet graphic.

Copy it onto a transparency.

Turn out the lights. Squeegee emulsion.

Flip and repeat on the back. Let dry.

Tape down the transparency.

Add the glass.

Expose under a 250-watt bulb.

Remove the glass and rinse thoroughly.

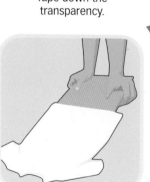
Slide a cardboard spacer into the shirt.

152 stain clothes on purpose

Squeegee ink over the design.

Lift the screen without smudging.

Hang your shirt to dry, you rock star!

tell me more

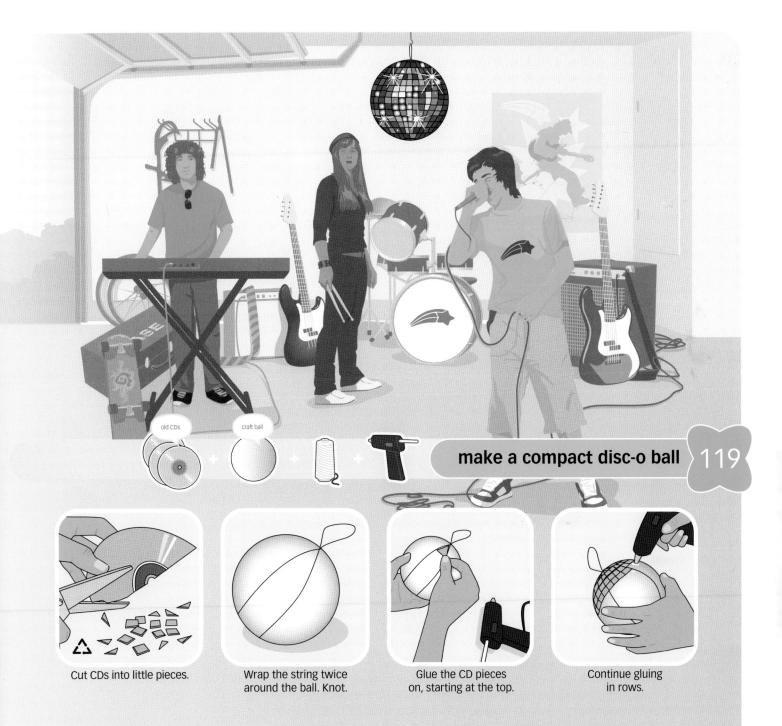

old CDs · craft ball

make a compact disc-o ball 119

Cut CDs into little pieces.

Wrap the string twice around the ball. Knot.

Glue the CD pieces on, starting at the top.

Continue gluing in rows.

explore

Straighten your arm away from your body, and hold your hand just below the sun (don't look right at the sun!). Now count the fingers between the sun and the horizon. Each finger counts for about fifteen minutes (so each hand represents one hour). The closer you are to the Earth's poles, the less accurate this trick will be.

Extend your arm fully in front of you to get a more accurate measurement.

58 **tell time with a potato**

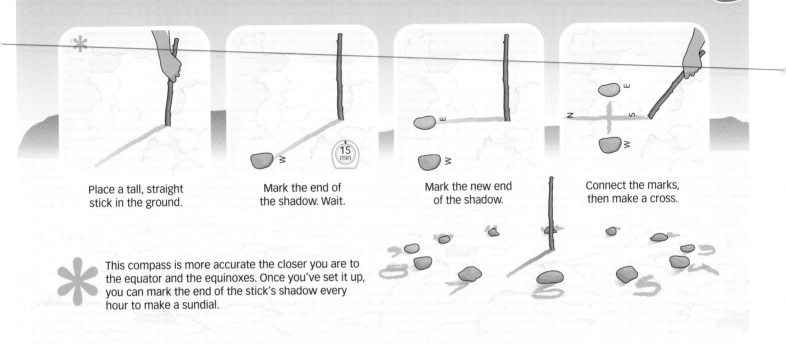

Place a tall, straight stick in the ground.

Mark the end of the shadow. Wait.

Mark the new end of the shadow.

Connect the marks, then make a cross.

This compass is more accurate the closer you are to the equator and the equinoxes. Once you've set it up, you can mark the end of the stick's shadow every hour to make a sundial.

The needle will align along the north-south axis. You'll have to use other clues, like the sun's position in the sky, to tell which end of the needle points north.

Make a windproof puddle.

Rub a needle against a magnet.

×50

Set the needle on a leaf in the puddle.

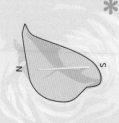

The needle aligns with the poles.

tell me more

locate the north star

First, locate the Big Dipper (also known as the Plough). Imagine a line between the two stars at the end of the Big Dipper's bowl. Extend that line five times, and you'll hit Polaris, the North Star (it's also the end of the Little Dipper's handle).

ursa major

polaris (north star)

ursa minor (little dipper)

big dipper (plough)

When you're in the Northern Hemisphere, finding the North Star is the handiest way to orient yourself at night.

spot pictures in the moon

The dark patches you see on the moon are ancient basins filled with hardened lava, or basalt. It's easy for us to see shapes in these basins, leading to the moon myths and stories many cultures have told for thousands of years.

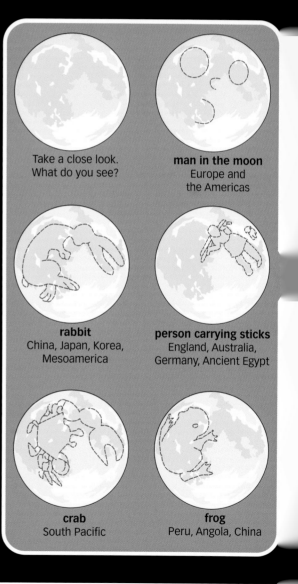

Take a close look. What do you see?

man in the moon
Europe and the Americas

rabbit
China, Japan, Korea, Mesoamerica

person carrying sticks
England, Australia, Germany, Ancient Egypt

crab
South Pacific

frog
Peru, Angola, China

The moon doesn't rotate as it circles the Earth, and the same part of the moon is always facing the sun. But we see different moon phases because we see the moon's bright face from a different angle each night.

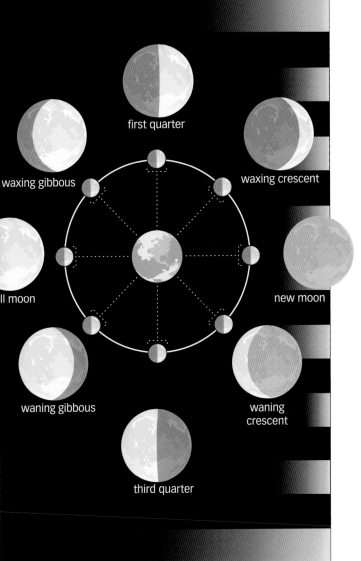

first quarter

waxing crescent

waxing gibbous

new moon

full moon

waning crescent

waning gibbous

third quarter

Want to find your way to the South Pole when you're in the Southern Hemisphere? Here's how!

rigil kent

hadar

south pole

southern cross (crux)

First, find the Southern Cross. Imagine a line down the long part of the cross, and lengthen that line four and a half times. Then find the bright stars Rigil Kent and Hadar just to the left of the Cross. Locate the point halfway between these two, and imagine a line from there to the end of the Southern Cross line. Bingo!

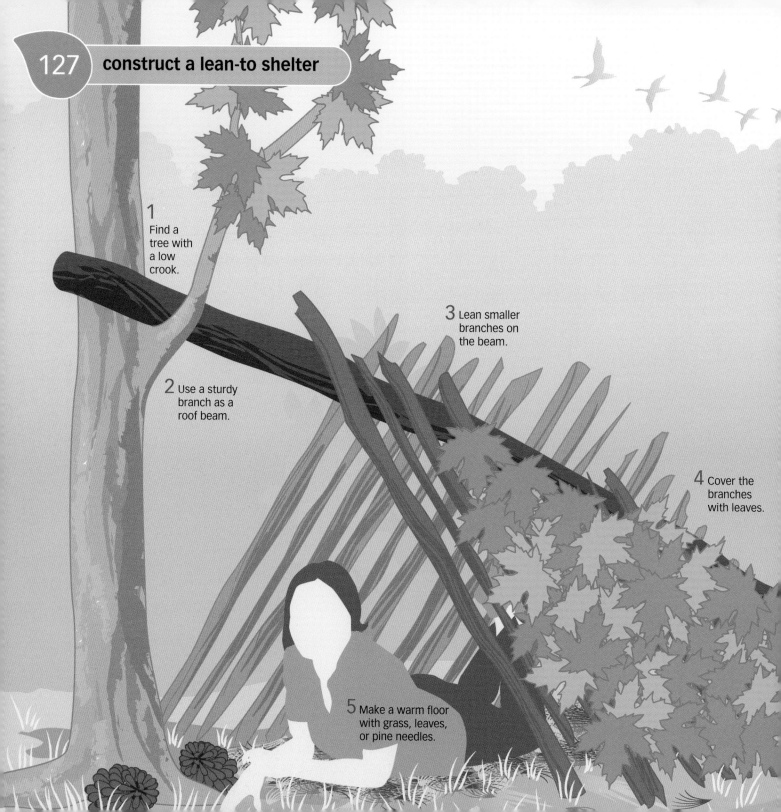

construct a lean-to shelter

1 Find a tree with a low crook.

2 Use a sturdy branch as a roof beam.

3 Lean smaller branches on the beam.

4 Cover the branches with leaves.

5 Make a warm floor with grass, leaves, or pine needles.

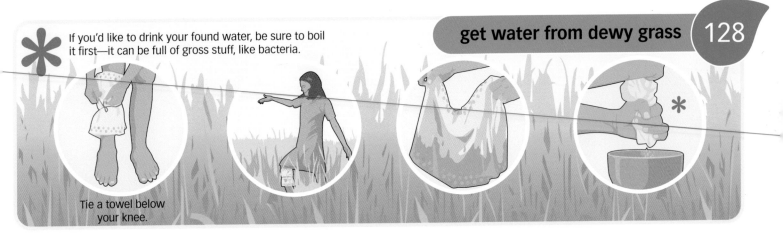

If you'd like to drink your found water, be sure to boil it first—it can be full of gross stuff, like bacteria.

Tie a towel below your knee.

tell me more

2 hr

dowse for water 29

4 hr

131 identify clouds

cirrus

cirrocumulus

cirrostratus

altocumulus

cumulonimbus

tell me more

predict a rainstorm

Many cultures believe that nature gives clues right before a rain. Watch for these signs from around the world, and you may never get caught in a surprise shower again!

2 mi
(3 km)

0 m
(0 km)

cumulus

contrail

stratus

stratocumulus

nimbostratus

Grass is dry in the morning.

Tree leaves flip over.

Cows lie down.

Crows fly low to the ground.

Spiders leave their webs.

The weather vane spins around twice.

Cats wash behind their ears.

Doors and windows are hard to open.

184 concoct chocolate anthills

Ants move their eggs to higher ground.

Time to hit the trail! Make these simple symbols with straw, sticks, or stones so that your friends can follow your path. Just remember: The last person down the path should take down the signs.

not the way

turn left

danger

tube-like with tapered ends

teardrop-shaped

pellets with bone and hair

raptors

felines

tell me more

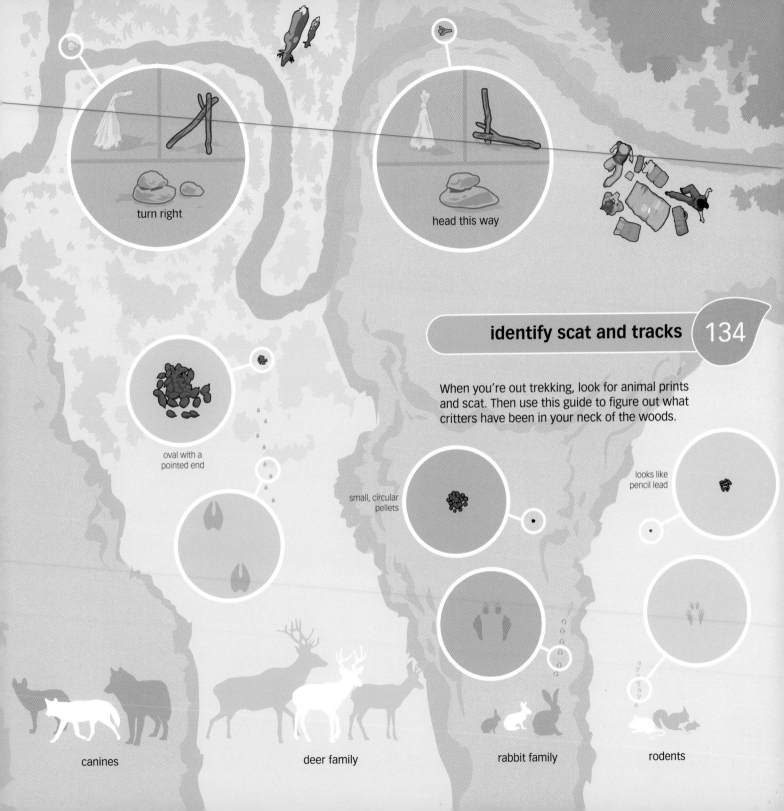

turn right

head this way

identify scat and tracks 134

When you're out trekking, look for animal prints and scat. Then use this guide to figure out what critters have been in your neck of the woods.

oval with a pointed end

small, circular pellets

looks like pencil lead

canines

deer family

rabbit family

rodents

135 learn dog body language

aggressive — raised fur, bared teeth

scared — hunched posture, tucked tail

relaxed — turned head, exposed belly

greeting — licking and sniffing, lowered tail

playful — open mouth, lowered front end

136 greet a new dog

May I pet your dog?

Check with the owner first.

Approach slowly from the front.

Let the dog sniff your fist.

Pet your new friend under the chin first.

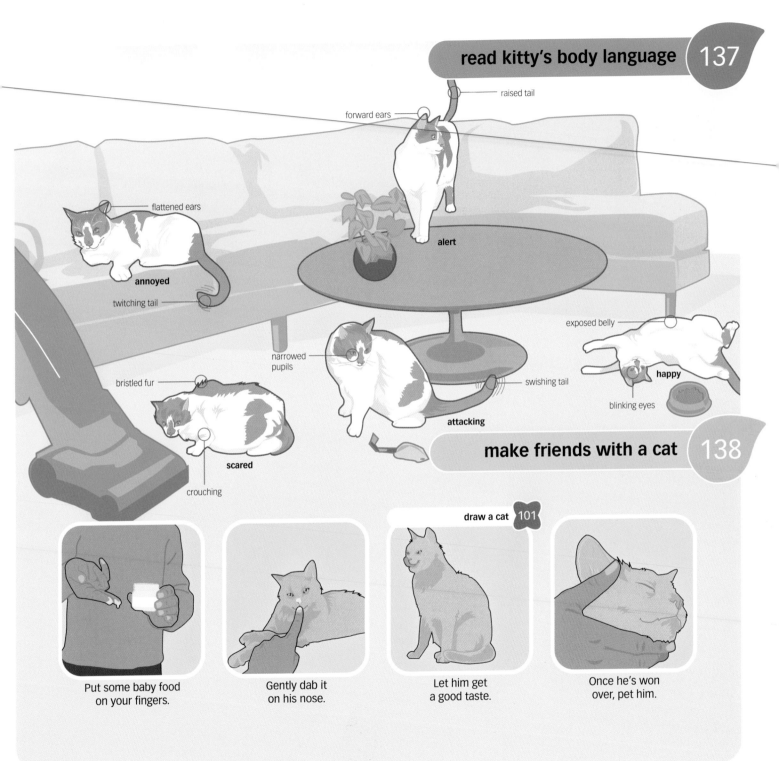

raised tail

forward ears

flattened ears

alert

annoyed

twitching tail

narrowed pupils

bristled fur

exposed belly

happy

swishing tail

blinking eyes

scared

crouching

attacking

draw a cat 101

Put some baby food
on your fingers.

Gently dab it
on his nose.

Let him get
a good taste.

Once he's won
over, pet him.

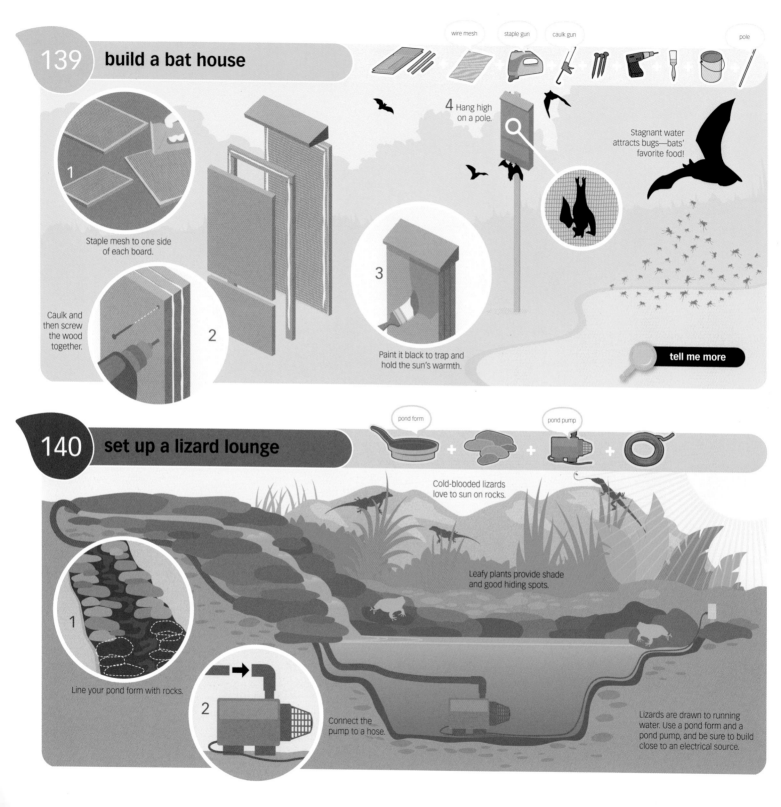

139 build a bat house

wire mesh
staple gun
caulk gun
pole

1 Staple mesh to one side of each board.

2 Caulk and then screw the wood together.

3 Paint it black to trap and hold the sun's warmth.

4 Hang high on a pole.

Stagnant water attracts bugs—bats' favorite food!

tell me more

140 set up a lizard lounge

pond form
+
+
pond pump
+

Cold-blooded lizards love to sun on rocks.

Leafy plants provide shade and good hiding spots.

1 Line your pond form with rocks.

2 Connect the pump to a hose.

Lizards are drawn to running water. Use a pond form and a pond pump, and be sure to build close to an electrical source.

hanging tray   silk flowers

Get colorful! You'll attract more butterflies with a rainbow of flowers.

To attract male butterflies, fill a bowl with sand, then add water, salt, and a little fruit juice.

Dig a hole and bury the bowl up to the rim.

Hang no higher than the yard's tallest flowers.

1 Decorate.

2 Add pieces of rotting fruit.

wood glue   eyebolt

Bees love flowers in bloom, especially fruit trees' blossoms.

Drill holes for the bees to lay their eggs in.

Hang your bee house in a protected spot.

dandelions

⅜ in (1 cm) wide

1 6 in (15 cm) deep

Mason bees need a source of mud, like the banks of a pond. They'll seal their nests with the mud and drink the freshwater.

tell me more

clover

2 7 in (18 cm)

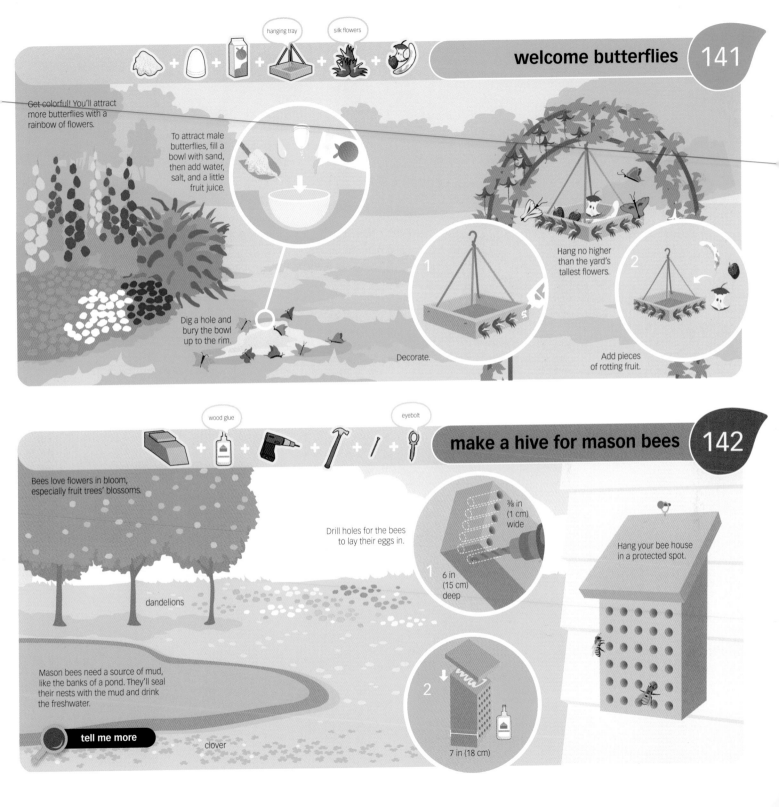

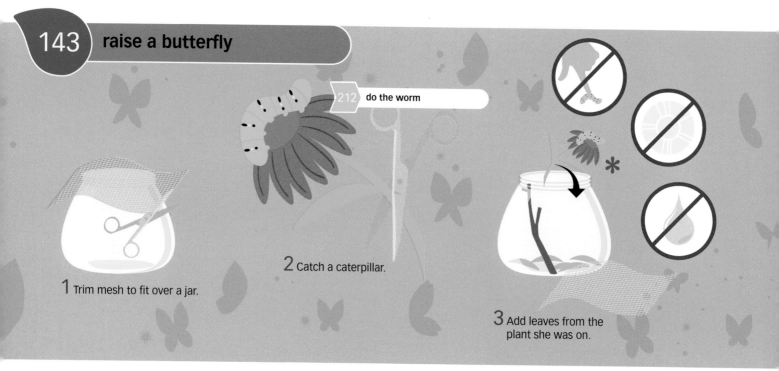

143 raise a butterfly

212 do the worm

1 Trim mesh to fit over a jar.

2 Catch a caterpillar.

3 Add leaves from the plant she was on.

144 start an ant farm

1 Find two nesting jars. Poke holes in the big lid.

2 Find an ant hill and locate the queen. No fire ants!

3 Funnel soil and worker ants into the large jar.

4 Add the queen and her eggs last.

You'll need a good field guide to help you identify your fuzzy friend, as well as tell you what she wants for breakfast, how damp she likes her jar, and when she'll be ready to fly away.

4 Insert fresh leaves and clean jar daily.

5 Spritz according to your guide and wait.

6 Add fresh flowers and an orange slice.

7 Release her where you found her.

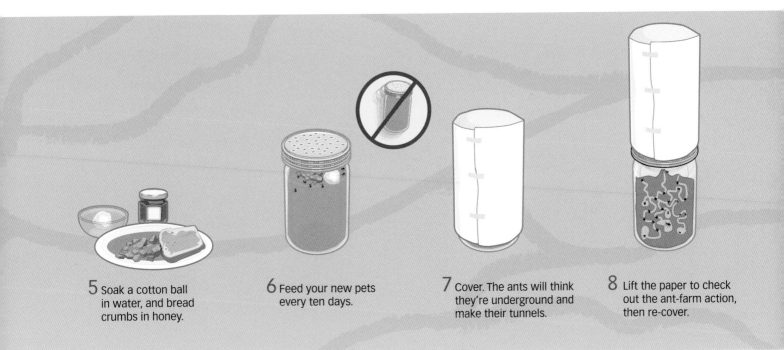

5 Soak a cotton ball in water, and bread crumbs in honey.

6 Feed your new pets every ten days.

7 Cover. The ants will think they're underground and make their tunnels.

8 Lift the paper to check out the ant-farm action, then re-cover.

spy on sea life

Cut the bottom off a
cup. Tape the edges.

Tape plastic wrap
over the mouth.

If you want to see what's going on in
deeper water, build the viewer with
a PVC pipe instead of a cup.

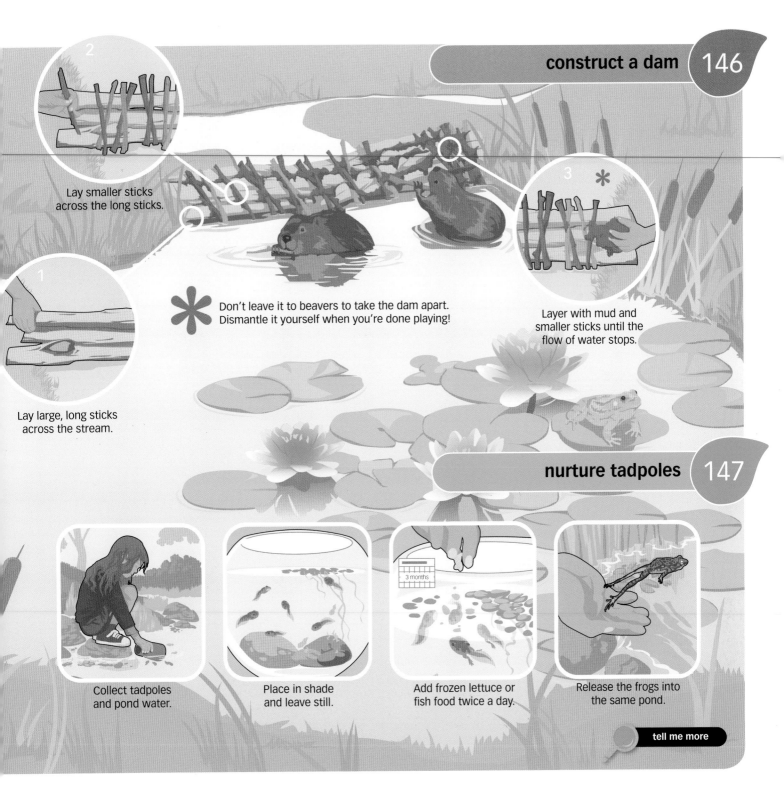

2 Lay smaller sticks across the long sticks.

3 * Layer with mud and smaller sticks until the flow of water stops.

1 Lay large, long sticks across the stream.

* Don't leave it to beavers to take the dam apart. Dismantle it yourself when you're done playing!

Collect tadpoles and pond water.

Place in shade and leave still.

Add frozen lettuce or fish food twice a day.

3 months

Release the frogs into the same pond.

tell me more

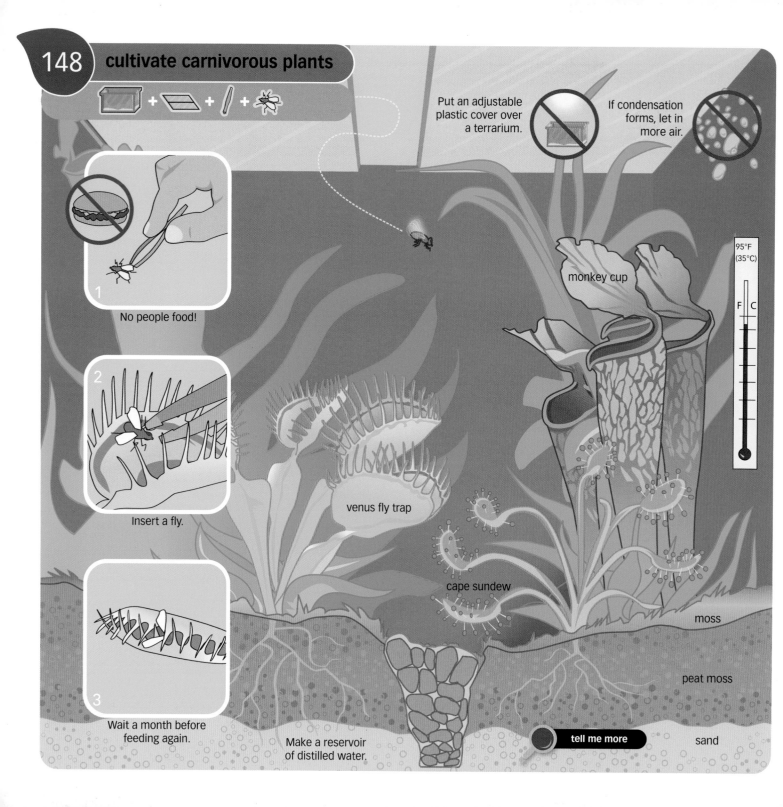

Put an adjustable plastic cover over a terrarium.

If condensation forms, let in more air.

monkey cup

95°F (35°C)

F | C

1

No people food!

2

Insert a fly.

3

Wait a month before feeding again.

venus fly trap

cape sundew

Make a reservoir of distilled water.

tell me more

moss

peat moss

sand

wood glue   clothesline

1. Give your gourd a good scrubbing.

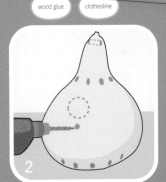

2. Drill holes. Cut a high entrance.

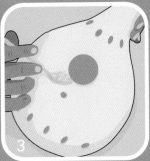

3. Scoop out the insides.

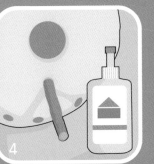

4. Glue in a perch.

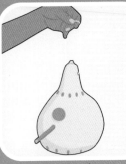

Thread a piece of clothesline.

6. Hang in early spring.

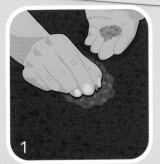

1. Plant the melon seeds.

2. Water.

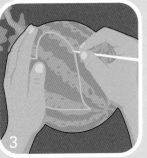

3. Etch shallow lines with a wood skewer.

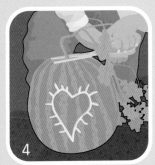

4. The melon will heal, revealing your art!

acid-free paper

1 Pluck some pretty flowers, stem and all.

2 Slice thicker flowers in half.

If you want to preserve your bouquets but keep them looking full, hang them upside down to dry.

3 Set on newspaper in a heavy book.

4 Fold the newspaper.

5 Close the book and add a weight.

6 Arrange on acid-free paper and frame.

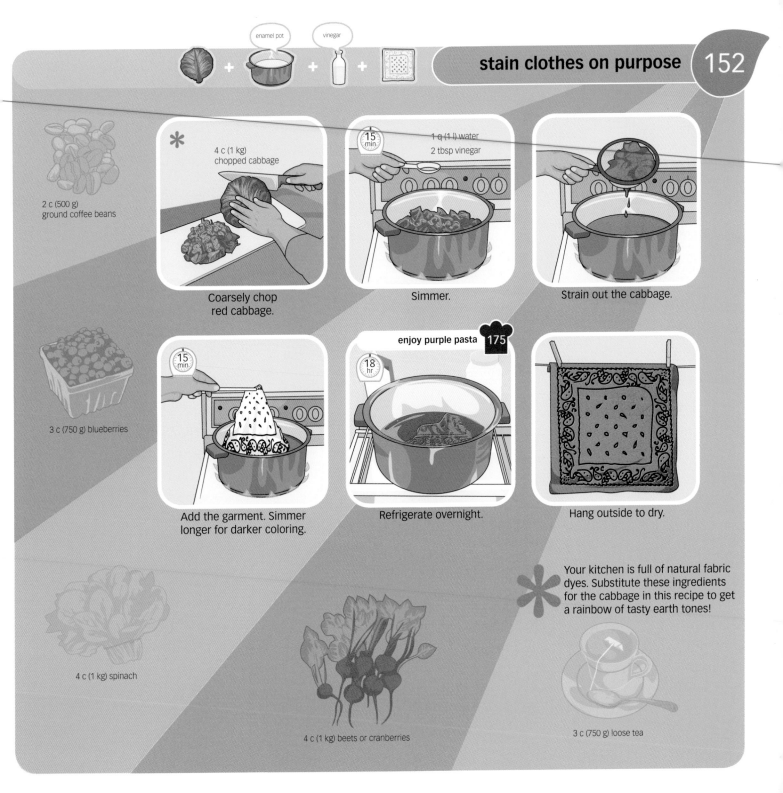

enamel pot

vinegar

2 c (500 g) ground coffee beans

3 c (750 g) blueberries

*
4 c (1 kg) chopped cabbage

Coarsely chop red cabbage.

15 min.
1 q (1 l) water
2 tbsp vinegar

Simmer.

Strain out the cabbage.

15 min.
Add the garment. Simmer longer for darker coloring.

enjoy purple pasta 175
18 hr.
Refrigerate overnight.

Hang outside to dry.

Your kitchen is full of natural fabric dyes. Substitute these ingredients for the cabbage in this recipe to get a rainbow of tasty earth tones!

4 c (1 kg) spinach

4 c (1 kg) beets or cranberries

3 c (750 g) loose tea

153 save poppy seeds

154 sprout an avocado pit

155 dry tomato seeds

156 pluck marigold seeds

Shred paper.

Fill a blender with equal
parts paper and water.

Blend at low speed until
you have mush.

Carefully stir in seeds.

Roll the pulp
onto a screen.

Turn on a fan to make the
paper dry more quickly.

Gently peel off
the dry paper.

Send a plantable
greeting card!

dig up a lost civilization

Choose (or invent!) a lost civilization and bury objects in your backyard that the society would have used. Then invite some friends to dig up your artifacts and piece together the life of your lost city, just like real archaeologists do!

1 Mark off a dig site.

2 Bury some "artifacts." Record their locations in a notebook.

3 Invite your friends over for some backyard archaeology.

4 Can they identify the ancient civilization you buried?

1. Pick an area with lots of foot traffic.

2. Prepare the plaster as the package instructs.

3. Carefully fill a footprint.

4. Let the plaster set, then remove.

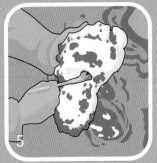

5. Brush off your fossil.

6. Try to figure out who made it!

cook

Use your favorite sweets (and your imagination) to make your own candy sushi. Fruit leather makes yummy nori, and gummy fish are great in nigiri. Keep it healthy with dried fruit stuffings (such as golden raisins or apricots), and get gooey with crisped rice treats for the rice rolls.

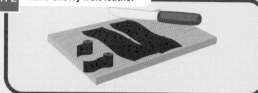

172 make chewy fruit leather

1 20 large marshmallows

3 tbsp butter

Melt together on medium-low heat.

2 3 c (700 g) rice cereal

Stir in crisped rice cereal.

3 10 min

Transfer to a greased pan to cool.

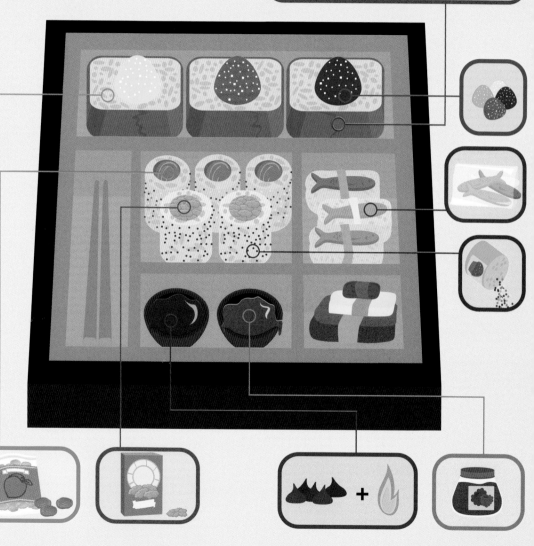

corn syrup   paper towel-wrapped fork   candy thermometer   vanilla extract   waxed paper

1¼ c (300 ml) corn syrup
2 c (450 g) sugar
¾ c (175 ml) water

Stir over low heat until sugar dissolves.

1 tsp salt

Raise heat. Wipe any crystals off the sides.

265°F (130°C)
2 tbsp butter

Remove when well heated. Add butter.

*

To make other flavors, substitute peppermint, almond, or lemon extract for the vanilla.

Divide. Wait until it's cool enough to handle.

12 in (30 cm)

Stretch one part with buttered hands.

Bring the ends together.

Grab the ends and loop. Stretch again.

*

3 drops food coloring

3 drops vanilla extract

Add flavor and color. Pull until taffy is stiff.

Cut with buttered scissors. Wrap.

two flavors twisted together

two flavors rolled in a pinwheel, then sliced

two flavors stacked, then sliced

 +  +  + 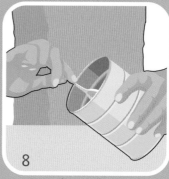 +

whipping cream · vanilla extract · 1 lb (450 g) coffee can · 3 lb (1.5 kg) coffee can · rock salt

1 c (250 ml)
milk

1 c (250 ml)
whipping cream

½ c (100 g)
sugar

½ tsp
vanilla extract

1

Pour the ingredients at
left into the smaller can.

2

Duct tape the lid
down securely.

3

Put the smaller can
into the big can.

4

Pack with lots of crushed
ice and a little rock salt.

5

Cover this lid with
a lot of duct tape.

202 master goalie moves

6

Roll, shake, or
kick the can.

7

Open the big can and
drain the melted ice.

8

Open the small can. Stir
and scrape the sides.

9

Tape. Repeat from step 3
until the ice cream is firm.

sparkling water

To make your own personal ice cream–soda concoction, try different flavor extracts in the ice cream and different fruits in the syrup.

1 c (225 g) berries
2 c (450 g) sugar
2 c (475 ml) water

1

Combine.

30 min

2

Cook over low heat until the sugar dissolves.

3

Strain and let cool.

4

Add lemon juice to taste.

5

Add ice. Fill a third of the way with syrup.

6

Top off with sparkling water, then stir.

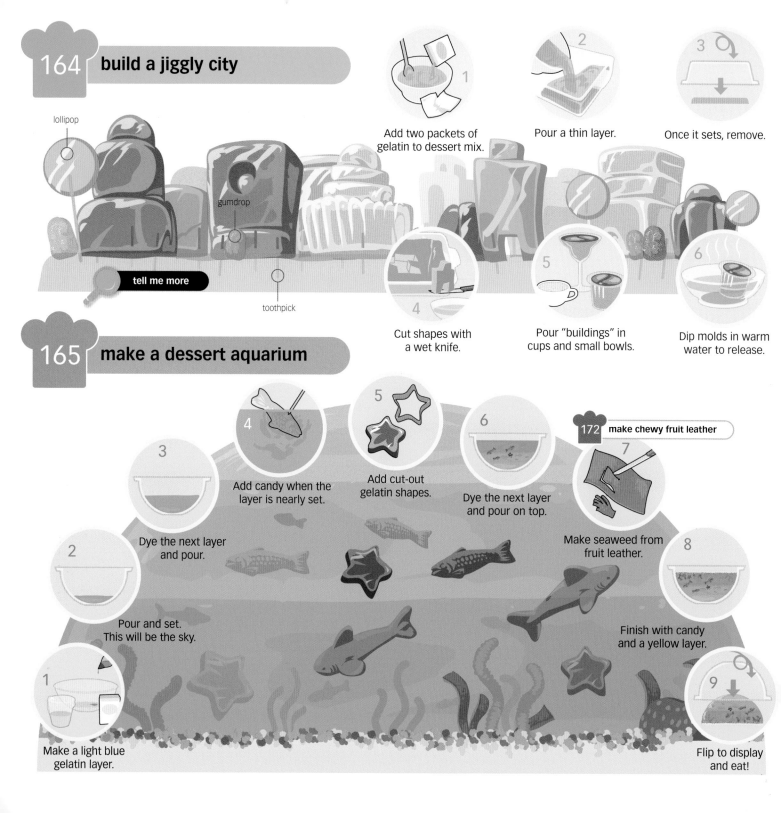

164 build a jiggly city

lollipop

gumdrop

tell me more

toothpick

1 Add two packets of gelatin to dessert mix.

2 Pour a thin layer.

3 Once it sets, remove.

4 Cut shapes with a wet knife.

5 Pour "buildings" in cups and small bowls.

6 Dip molds in warm water to release.

165 make a dessert aquarium

1 Make a light blue gelatin layer.

2 Pour and set. This will be the sky.

3 Dye the next layer and pour.

4 Add candy when the layer is nearly set.

5 Add cut-out gelatin shapes.

6 Dye the next layer and pour on top.

172 make chewy fruit leather

7 Make seaweed from fruit leather.

8 Finish with candy and a yellow layer.

9 Flip to display and eat!

sugar-cookie dough

parchment paper

Roll out prepared cookie dough.

Use a flour-coated cookie cutter to cut out cookies.

Set on parchment paper and cut holes.

Fill a bag with hard candy. Crush with a rolling pin.

Cut the tip off the plastic bag.

Sprinkle the crushed candies into the holes.

Bake until light brown.

350°F
175°C
8 min

Let the sun shine through!

tell me more

167 separate an egg

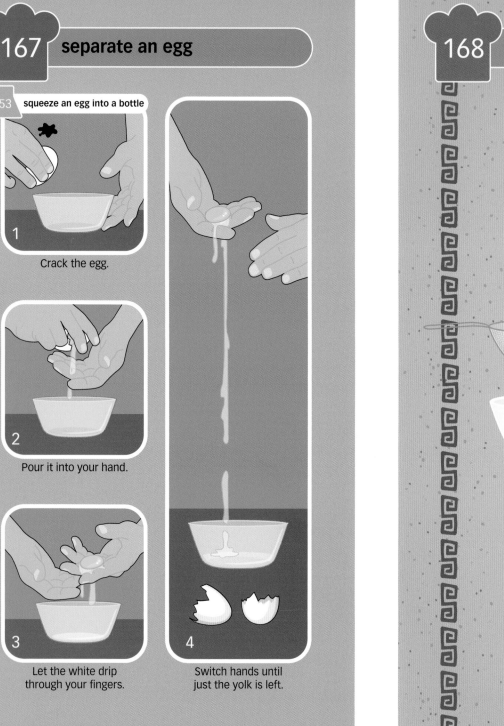

53 squeeze an egg into a bottle

1 Crack the egg.

2 Pour it into your hand.

3 Let the white drip through your fingers.

4 Switch hands until just the yolk is left.

168 make fortune-cookie dough

1 egg white
⅛ tsp vanilla extract

1 Whisk together.

2 Sift together into another bowl.

¼ c (35 g) flour
¼ c (50 g) sugar
pinch of salt

3 Combine and mix with a wooden spoon.

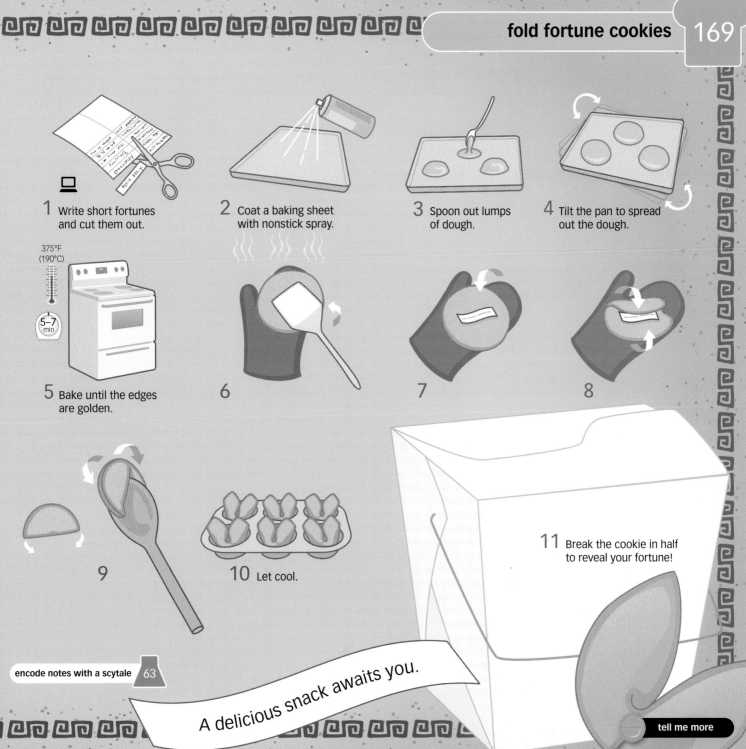

1 Write short fortunes and cut them out.

2 Coat a baking sheet with nonstick spray.

3 Spoon out lumps of dough.

4 Tilt the pan to spread out the dough.

375°F (190°C)

5–7 min

5 Bake until the edges are golden.

6

7

8

9

10 Let cool.

11 Break the cookie in half to reveal your fortune!

encode notes with a scytale 63

A delicious snack awaits you.

tell me more

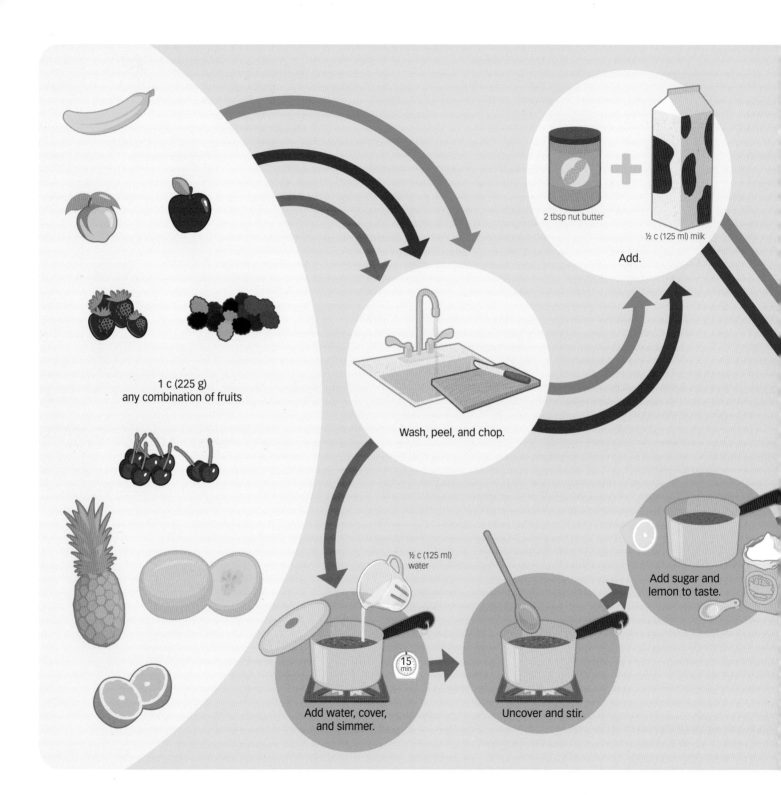

1 c (225 g)
any combination of fruits

2 tbsp nut butter

½ c (125 ml) milk

Add.

Wash, peel, and chop.

½ c (125 ml) water

Add water, cover, and simmer.

15 min.

Uncover and stir.

Add sugar and lemon to taste.

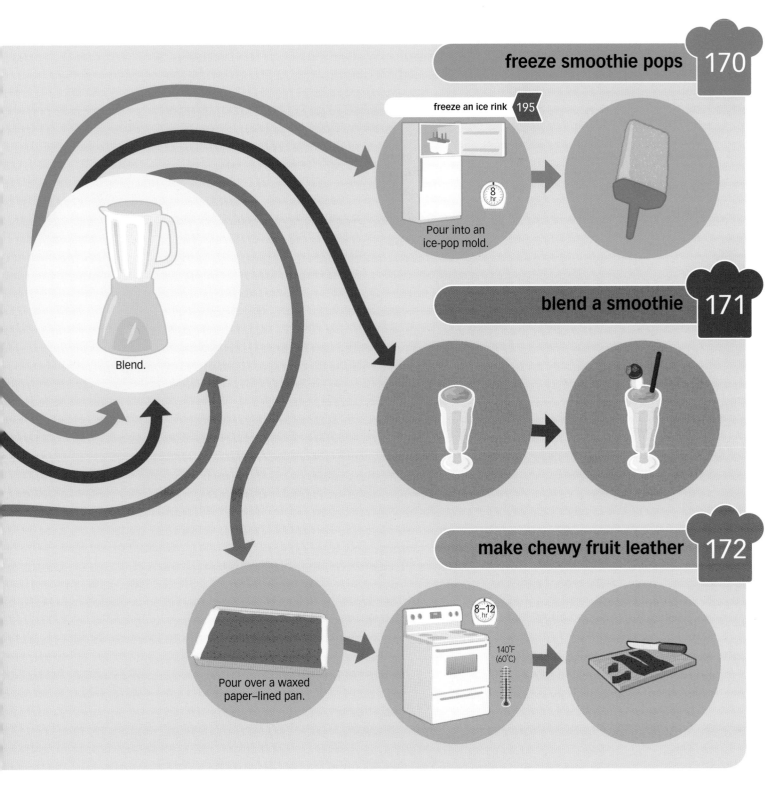

freeze an ice rink 195

freeze smoothie pops 170

Pour into an
ice-pop mold.

8 hr

blend a smoothie 171

make chewy fruit leather 172

Blend.

Pour over a waxed
paper–lined pan.

8–12 hr

140°F
(60°C)

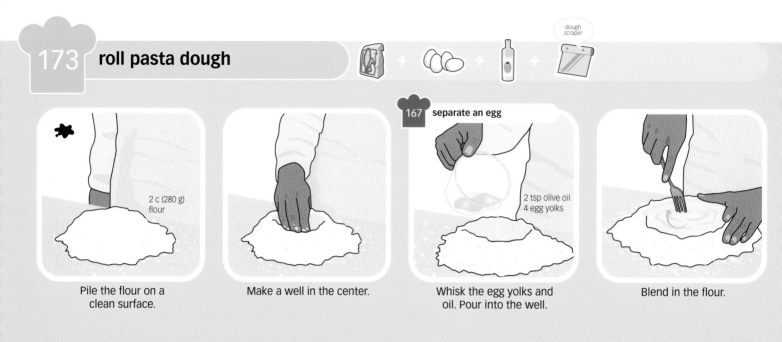

173 roll pasta dough

Pile the flour on a clean surface.

Make a well in the center.

167 separate an egg

2 tsp olive oil
4 egg yolks

Whisk the egg yolks and oil. Pour into the well.

2 c (280 g) flour

Blend in the flour.

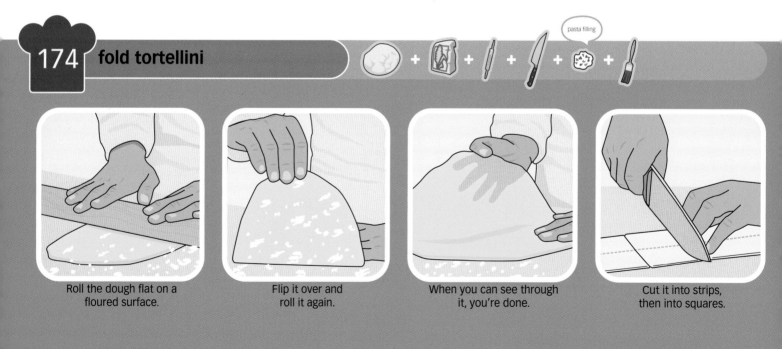

174 fold tortellini

pasta filling

Roll the dough flat on a floured surface.

Flip it over and roll it again.

When you can see through it, you're done.

Cut it into strips, then into squares.

Roll all the flour
into the dough.

Knead on a floured surface
until the dough is smooth.

Cut into quarters.

Flatten each
quarter into a disk.

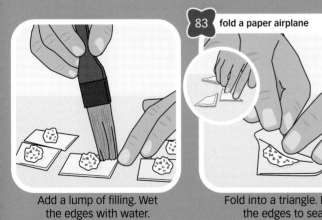

Add a lump of filling. Wet
the edges with water.

83 fold a paper airplane

Fold into a triangle. Press
the edges to seal.

Wrap the corners around
and press together.

Gently add to boiling
water. Cook and serve.

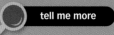

tell me more

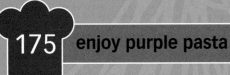

175 enjoy purple pasta

Cut the tops off the beets and discard.

Set the beets top-down in a little water.

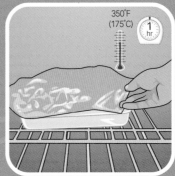

350°F
(175°C)

1 hr

Cover with foil and bake.

Let the beets cool, then peel. Reserve the juice.

Dice one. Save the rest for another recipe.

10 min

Cook the pasta in boiling water.

Drain.

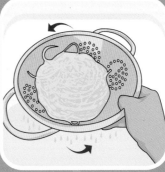

1 tbsp beet juice

Toss with diced beets, beet juice, and butter.

Lame celery snacks got you down? Cut the ends off your stalks and set them in colored water. Place them in the fridge, and check on them daily to see how much dye has traveled up the stems. Pretty soon, you'll have the brightest veggies on the block!

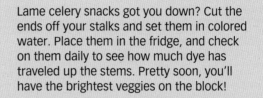

20 drops food coloring

tell me more

twist up soft pretzels

active dry yeast · vegetable oil · plastic wrap · coarse salt

1 tsp sugar
1¼ c (300 ml) warm water
10 min
4 tsp yeast

Mix yeast, sugar, and warm water. Let sit.

1½ tsp table salt
5 c (700 kg) flour
½ c (100 g) sugar

In another bowl, mix flour, sugar, and salt.

1 tbsp vegetable oil

Make a well. Add the yeast mix and oil.

7 min

Knead into dough. Add water if it's dry.

Oil a bowl. Add dough and turn to coat.

1 hr

Cover and set aside to rise.

4 c (1 l) hot water
½ c (100 g) baking soda

Dissolve baking soda in hot water.

Turn risen dough onto a floured surface.

Roll it into ropes and twist to make shapes.

Dip each into the baking soda water.

Set on greased baking sheet. Add salt.

450°F (230°C)
8 min

Bake until golden brown.

vinegar   pickling spice

Seed the pepper and
cut the veggies.

1 green pepper
2 cucumbers
1 red onion
2 cloves garlic

Put them in
a clean jar.

Combine sugar and
vinegar over low heat.

1 c (250 ml)
white vinegar
2 c (400 g) sugar

Add seasoning. Cook
until sugar dissolves.

1 tbsp pickling spice
1 tsp salt

Remove the marinade
from heat and let sit.

1 hr

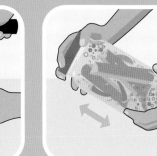

Cover the veggies
with the marinade.

Seal, then shake
the jar to mix.

Let marinate in
the fridge.

Pickling isn't just for cucumbers! Try this recipe
with other vegetables, or even a hard-boiled egg.

Whoever said you shouldn't play with your food was wrong. You can turn that boring lunch into a team of crazy creatures, like a mouse made with scoops of steamed brown rice, or a hot-dog dog with a waggin' bean-sprout tail. Use toothpicks or pretzel sticks to build your edible creations.

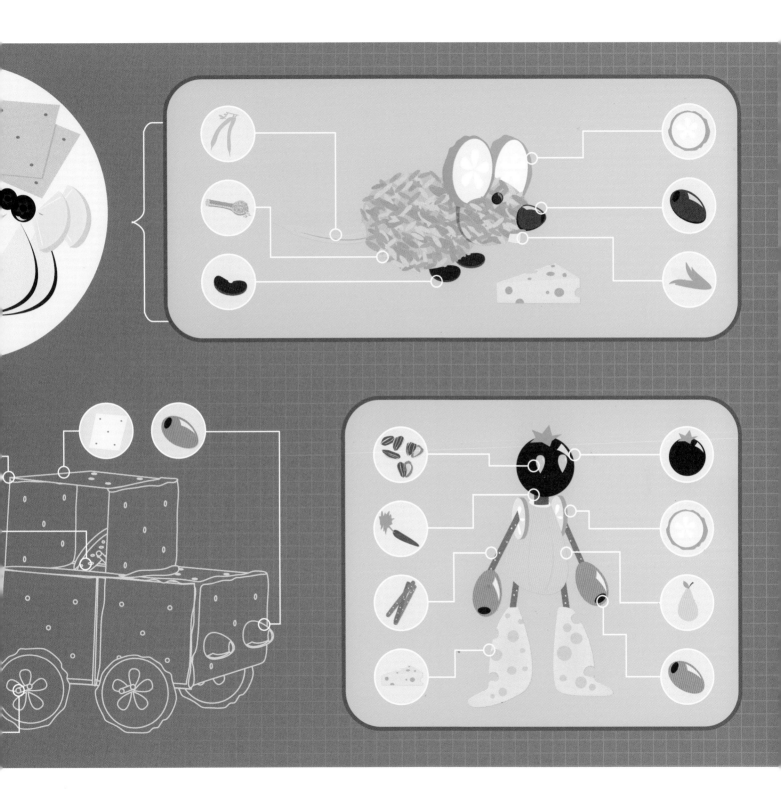

180 roast veggies in the wild

1 Cut the veggies into equal-size pieces.

2 Toss with olive oil, salt, and pepper.

3 Put the veggies on a square of tinfoil.

4 Fold into a packet.

5 Add to coals. Flip after five minutes.

10 min

6 Unwrap and enjoy!

181 grill cheese on a stick

130 **drink from a tree branch**

1 Scrape the bark off part of a forked stick.

×2

2 Butter one side of each bread slice.

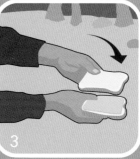

3 Put cheese between the unbuttered sides.

5 min

4 Hold over the fire.

5 When it browns, move away and flip.

5 min

6 Grill the other side.

+ cake mix + egg + vegetable oil + foil

1 Cut off the oranges' tops, then hollow out.

2 Prepare the cake batter.

3 Fill each halfway with batter. Add the tops.

4 Wrap each in foil.

5 35 min Place them in coals and turn often.

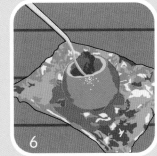

6 Unwrap and enjoy your campfire cake!

cinnamon + sugar + apple + peeler + knife + oven mitt

1 tbsp cinnamon
½ c (100 g) sugar

1 Combine cinnamon and sugar.

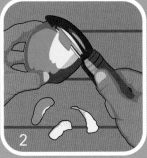

2 Peel an apple.

3 Place the apple on the end of a stick.

4 3–5 min Soften it over the fire, turning often.

5 Roll the apple through the sugar mix.

6 5–7 min Heat until the sugar melts.

chocolate + vanilla bean + crispy chow mein noodles + parchment paper

Melt chocolate in a double boiler.

Add vanilla seeds.

144 start an ant farm

Stir in ants and noodles.

Spoon onto parchment paper. Cool in the fridge.

locust

grasshopper

cricket

Don't get all bug-eyed! Many cultures think bugs are tasty treats—and great sources of protein and fiber. You can cook up crickets, ants, even spiders! Look for these yummy insects at a pet-supply or a bait store (or order them online), and ask about the preparation method for your bug of choice.

beetle

bird spider

gelatin + cocoa powder + oatmeal + raisins + cooking spray

1 package
unflavored gelatin
15 min

¼ c (60 ml)
applesauce

Mix over low heat.

Add two pinches
cocoa powder.

Some oatmeal and a few
raisins add nasty texture.

Coat a large plate with
nonstick spray.

2 hr

Spoon the gross mixture
onto the plate to cool.

booby-trap a bathroom 43

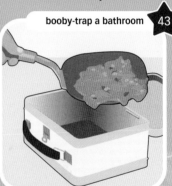

Remove the barf and hide
it somewhere clever.

move

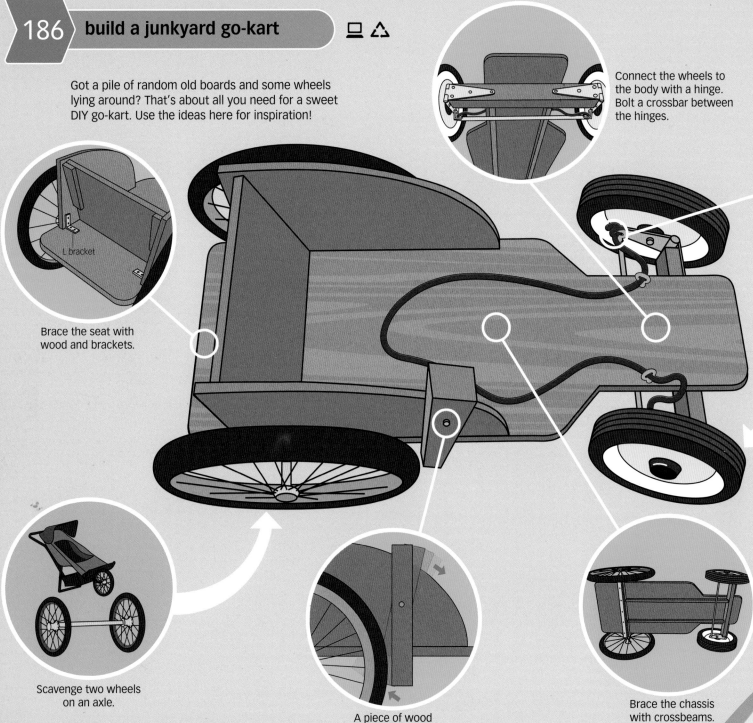

Got a pile of random old boards and some wheels lying around? That's about all you need for a sweet DIY go-kart. Use the ideas here for inspiration!

Connect the wheels to the body with a hinge. Bolt a crossbar between the hinges.

L bracket

Brace the seat with wood and brackets.

Scavenge two wheels on an axle.

A piece of wood pivots to brake.

Brace the chassis with crossbeams.

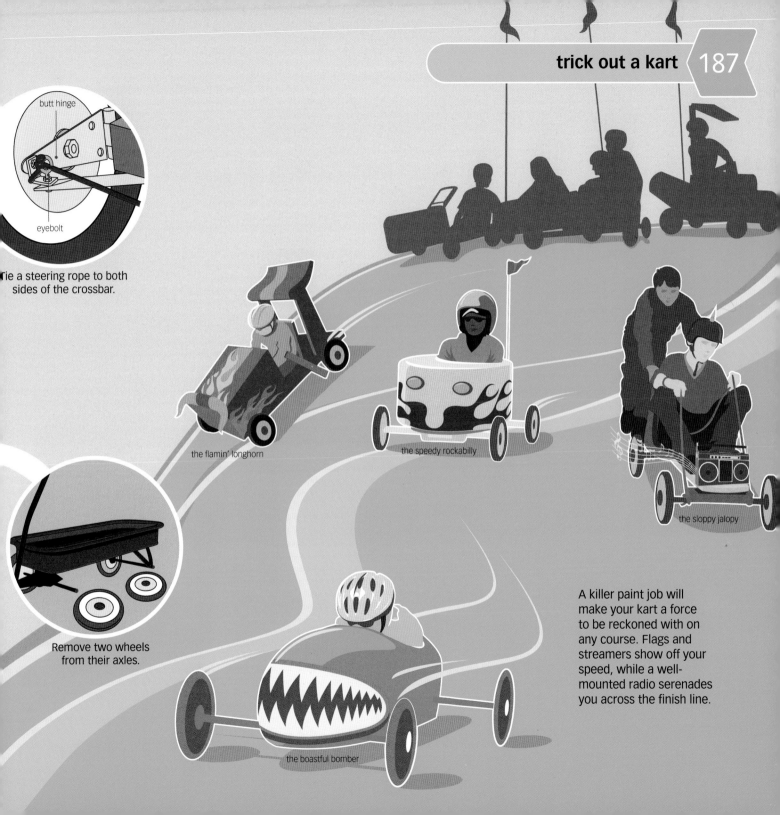

butt hinge

eyebolt

Tie a steering rope to both sides of the crossbar.

the flamin' longhorn

the speedy rockabilly

the sloppy jalopy

Remove two wheels from their axles.

A killer paint job will make your kart a force to be reckoned with on any course. Flags and streamers show off your speed, while a well-mounted radio serenades you across the finish line.

the boastful bomber

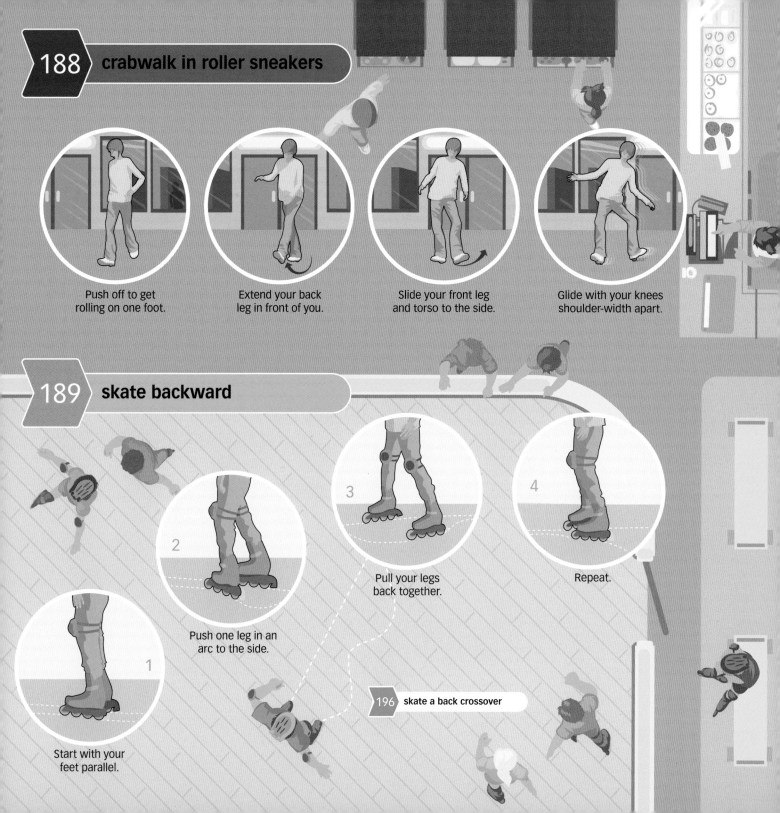

188 crabwalk in roller sneakers

Push off to get rolling on one foot.

Extend your back leg in front of you.

Slide your front leg and torso to the side.

Glide with your knees shoulder-width apart.

189 skate backward

2 Push one leg in an arc to the side.

3 Pull your legs back together.

4 Repeat.

1 Start with your feet parallel.

196 skate a back crossover

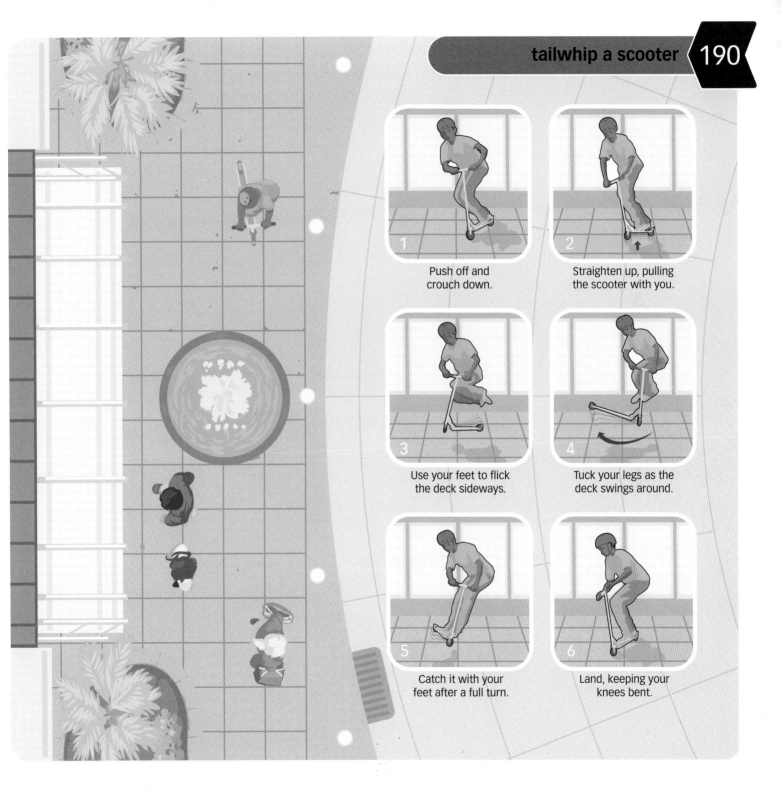

1. Push off and crouch down.

2. Straighten up, pulling the scooter with you.

3. Use your feet to flick the deck sideways.

4. Tuck your legs as the deck swings around.

5. Catch it with your feet after a full turn.

6. Land, keeping your knees bent.

1 Ollie up onto a ramp.

2 Straddle the back truck over the edge. Point the nose to the far side.

3 Grind down the ramp's edge. Ollie off.

1 Crouch with one foot at the center and one at the tail end.

2 Kick the tail down. Drag your front foot up the board.

3 **do a stuntman vault**

3 Lift both knees toward your chest.

4 Land it!

When you're first learning to skateboard, ride on the grass with a parent watching. Always wear a helmet and wrist guards. With lots of practice, you can move up to the adventurous tricks shown here!

4 Land it with both feet over the trucks (the wheel sets).

4 Land with your feet over the trucks.

3 Bring both feet above the board as it turns.

2 Leap. Kick the board into a sick spin.

1 Squat down to gather momentum.

1 Dive into a handstand. Grab the board on the outside of both trucks.

2 Bend your knees. Jerk the board to spin it.

3 Release it. Pull your legs under your hips.

4 Land with both feet over the trucks.

Find a level spot and pack snow into walls.

7 in (18 cm)

Pour water over walls and let it freeze.

Lay down a tarp with plenty of overhang.

2 ft (60 cm)

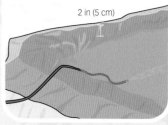

Add water and let it set for a few freezing nights.

2 in (5 cm)

196 skate a back crossover

Start skating backward. Gather momentum.

Cross your right foot in front of your left.

Bring your left foot to the side.

Repeat, starting with your right foot.

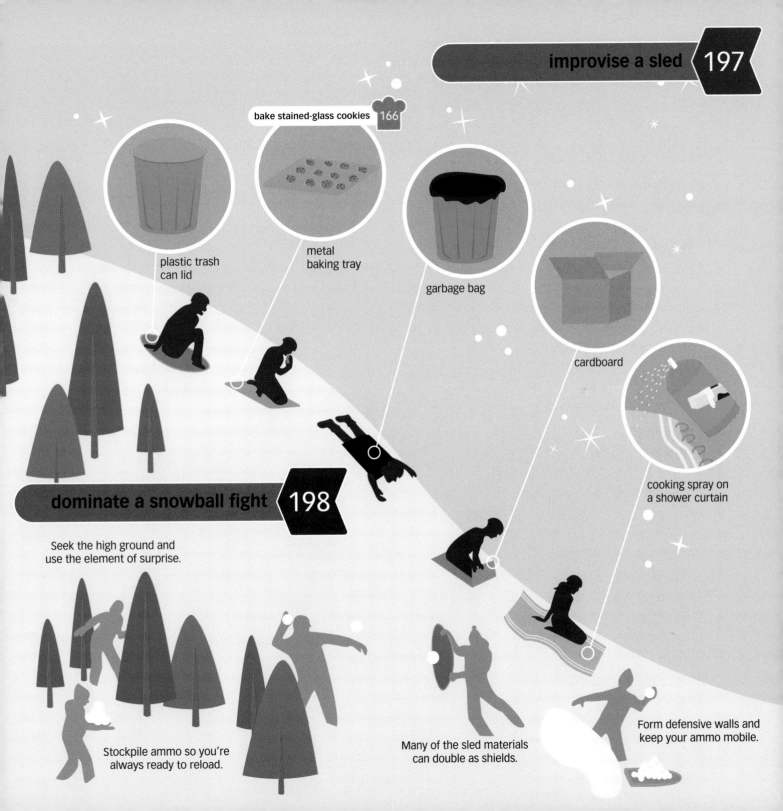

improvise a sled **197**

bake stained-glass cookies **166**

plastic trash
can lid

metal
baking tray

garbage bag

cardboard

cooking spray on
a shower curtain

dominate a snowball fight **198**

Seek the high ground and
use the element of surprise.

Stockpile ammo so you're
always ready to reload.

Many of the sled materials
can double as shields.

Form defensive walls and
keep your ammo mobile.

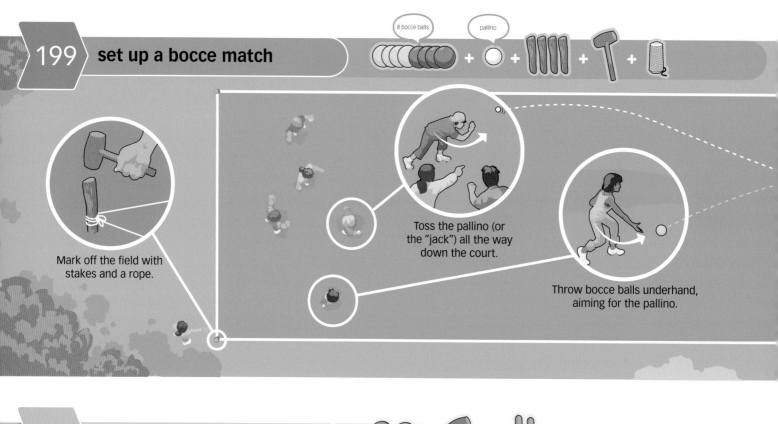

199 set up a bocce match

8 bocce balls + pallino + + +

Mark off the field with stakes and a rope.

Toss the pallino (or the "jack") all the way down the court.

Throw bocce balls underhand, aiming for the pallino.

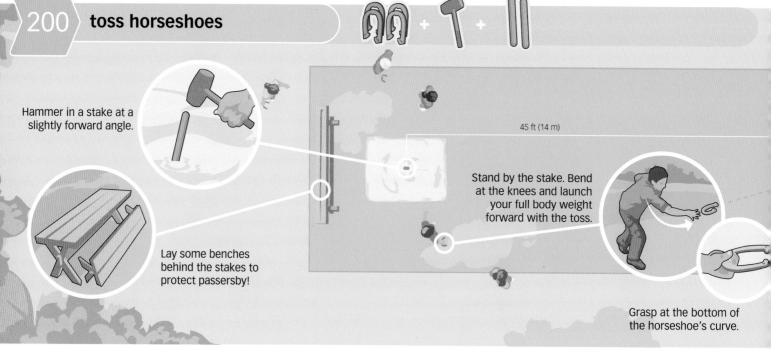

200 toss horseshoes

+ +

Hammer in a stake at a slightly forward angle.

Lay some benches behind the stakes to protect passersby!

45 ft (14 m)

Stand by the stake. Bend at the knees and launch your full body weight forward with the toss.

Grasp at the bottom of the horseshoe's curve.

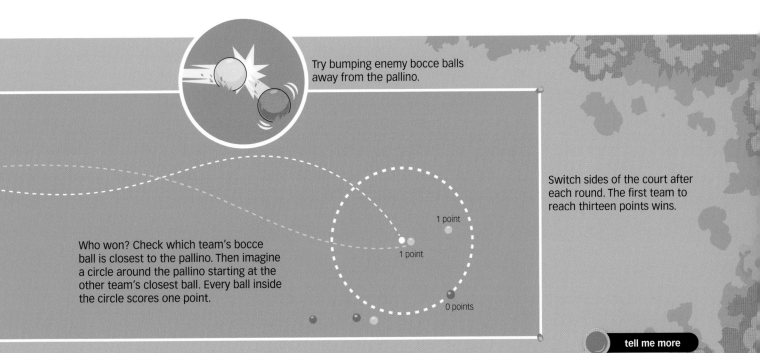

Try bumping enemy bocce balls away from the pallino.

Switch sides of the court after each round. The first team to reach thirteen points wins.

Who won? Check which team's bocce ball is closest to the pallino. Then imagine a circle around the pallino starting at the other team's closest ball. Every ball inside the circle scores one point.

1 point

1 point

0 points

tell me more

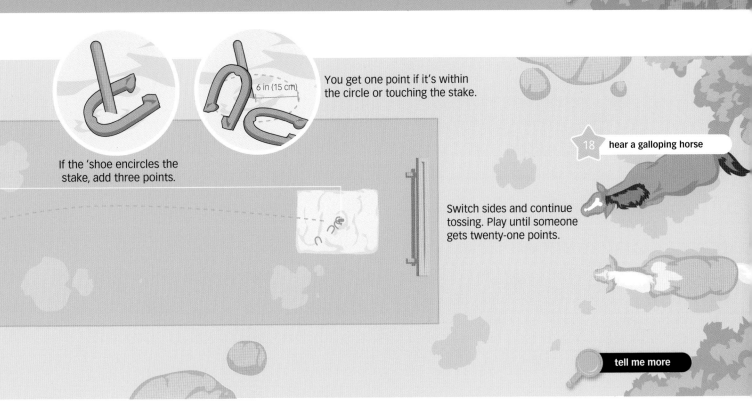

You get one point if it's within the circle or touching the stake.

If the 'shoe encircles the stake, add three points.

6 in (15 cm)

Switch sides and continue tossing. Play until someone gets twenty-one points.

18 hear a galloping horse

tell me more

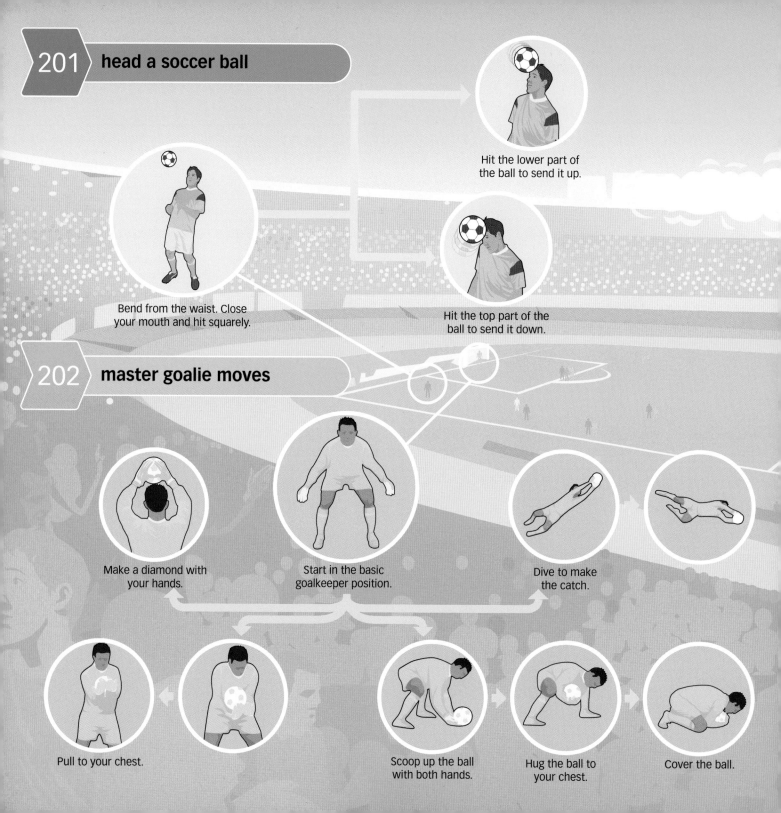

201 head a soccer ball

Bend from the waist. Close your mouth and hit squarely.

Hit the lower part of the ball to send it up.

Hit the top part of the ball to send it down.

202 master goalie moves

Make a diamond with your hands.

Start in the basic goalkeeper position.

Dive to make the catch.

Pull to your chest.

Scoop up the ball with both hands.

Hug the ball to your chest.

Cover the ball.

1. Put index and middle fingers on the seam.

2. Hide your hand to conceal your grip.

3. Shift to your back foot. Angle your front.

4. Wind up using your front leg and arm.

5. Release with your fingers over the ball.

6. Follow through after you throw.

1. Stand at the free-throw line.

2. Crouch down. Keep your knees loose.

3. Focus on the backboard.

4. Put one hand on the ball's side to guide it.

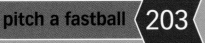

5. Straighten up. Flick your wrists.

6. Swish!

205 ride a boogie board

1 Wear flippers for speed.

2 Swim past the wave break.

3 Watch for a perfect wave.

4 Swim hard in front of the wave.

206 bodysurf a wave

Swim out beyond the wave break.

Wait for a wave, then swim in front of it.

Swim to the side of the break.

Take a deep breath. Steer with your arms.

5 Use your hands and shoulders to steer.

6 Ride the curl!

Gnarly!

Riding in the "curl" (perpendicular to the direction the wave is heading) takes practice! Start by riding the wave straight into the beach.

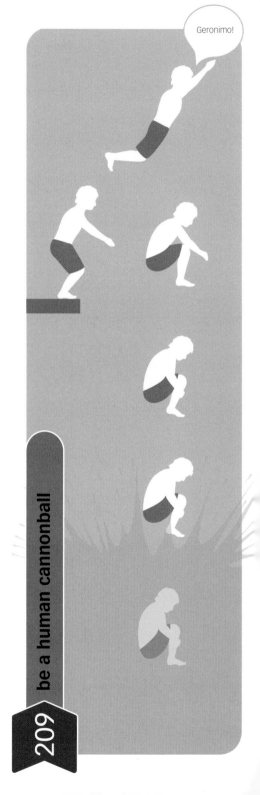

207 sail into a swan dive

12 ft (4 m)

208 do a jackknife dive

209 be a human cannonball

Geronimo!

Swim toward the wall. Tuck your head.

Continue to somersault.

Plant your feet against the wall.

Push off, turning your body.

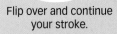

Flip over and continue your stroke.

* Float flat on your back.

Fold in half, sculling with your arms.

Point your head toward the bottom.

Raise your arms above your head.

Let your body sink down.

* The barracuda is one of many moves used in the sport of synchronized swimming. Try doing it with friends at the same time to get the full effect!

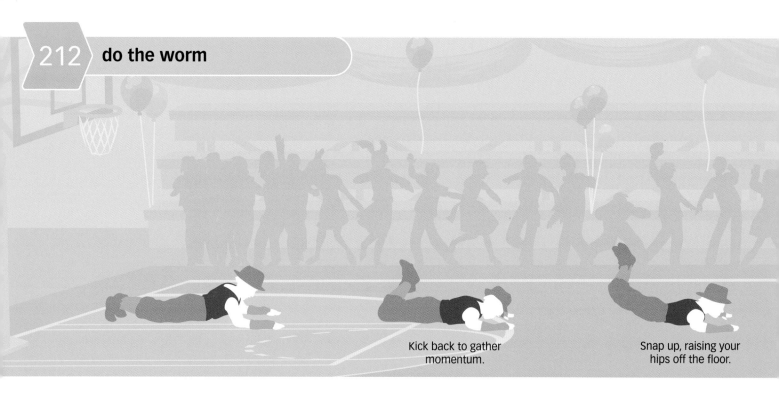

212 do the worm

Kick back to gather momentum.

Snap up, raising your hips off the floor.

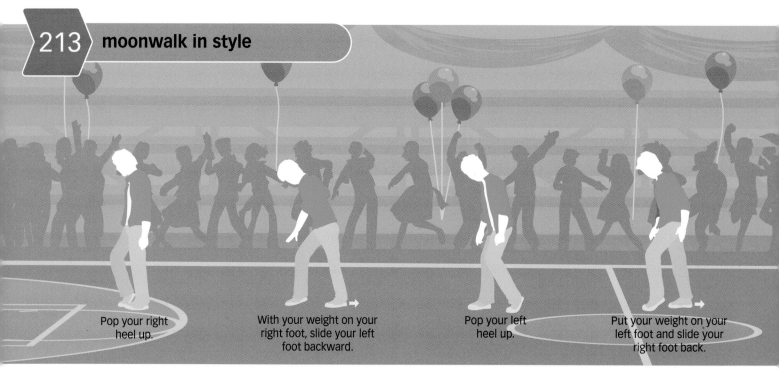

213 moonwalk in style

Pop your right heel up.

With your weight on your right foot, slide your left foot backward.

Pop your left heel up.

Put your weight on your left foot and slide your right foot back.

Land on your toes
and push up.

50 do a rock-star jump

Repeat, starting with
your right heel up.

Slide your left foot
back. You got it!

Pivot and . . .

. . . moonwalk back
the other way.

214 | stand on your head

Clear away furniture.
Kneel down.

Put your head and
hands down.

Straighten your legs.

Set one knee on
your elbow.

Put the other knee
on the other elbow.

Raise both legs
into the air.

215 | walk on your hands

Stand in an open,
flat area.

Dive forward. Kick
one foot in the air.

Kick off with your
other foot.

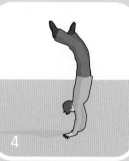

Swing both legs up.
Bend your knees.

"Step" one
hand forward.

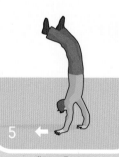

Bring the other
hand forward.

Want to turn head over heels? Practice each phase until you've got it down, then move to the next. Take it slow!

twist up soft pretzels 177

1. Gently stretch into a bridge position.

2. "Walk" your hands down a wall into a bridge. Then try it without the wall.

3. Walk up the wall, then kick over.

4. Practice kicking over without the wall. Tighten your stomach muscles.

5. Put it all together, and tumble off into the distance.

217 ace a cherry drop

Grab the bar. Bring your toes up to touch the bar.

Place your legs over the bar.

Hang from the bar by your knees.

Start swinging back and forth to build momentum.

 When you're cruising for a perfect high bar, make sure there's a soft surface underneath. You'll also need a spotter to help you practice these moves—they're more fun with an audience anyway!

218 skin the cat

Seize the bar and kick back to build momentum.

Swing your legs up. Bring both under the bar.

Let your legs drop down.

Let go, and land with your knees bent.

Keep swinging—you want to have a lot of speed!

Release the bar by unbending your knees.

Tuck your legs underneath you.

Nail your landing with your knees bent.

* Start upright on the bar.

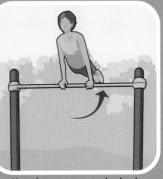

Keeping your arms locked, swing your legs back.

Sweep your legs around the bar in a circle.

Presto! You're right back where you started.

Crouch low.

Hop up, pulling the handlebars with you.

Point your toes down. Keep pulling up!

Tuck your legs up to raise the back wheel.

Land it!

* Don't have a dirt-bike course nearby? Practice your tricks on the grass to avoid gnarly skinned knees. When you feel confident, move up to the pavement!

Start pedaling slowly.

Push one pedal down hard and lean backward.

Lean back farther and pull up on the handlebars.

Rock out! Keep your balance.

Lean forward and push the handlebars down.

Set the front wheel down.

drill · rubber tube · mulch

Start with a sturdy tree.

10 in (25 cm)
9 ft (3 m)

Clean an old tire.

Drill three holes
for drainage.

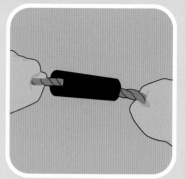

Add tubing to protect the
tree and prevent fraying.

Ask an adult to place
the rope.

25 tie a knot one-handed

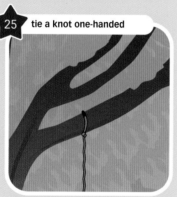

Have an adult tie the
rope securely.

Hang with the drainage
holes at the bottom.

Add some mulch for
softer landings.

tell me more

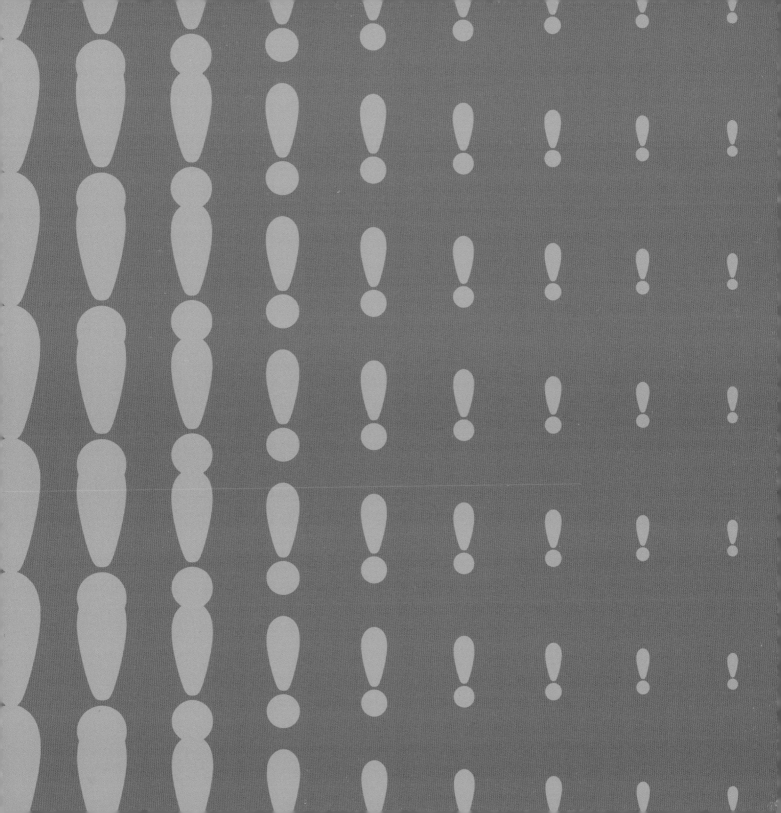

tell me more

Pssst! Want to know more about a project in this book? This handy section is full of trivia, history, and extra expert advice that will help you tackle certain activities or better understand what's so awesome about them.

18 hear a galloping horse

Before television, people listened to drama or comedy shows on the radio. To make these stories sound realistic and action-packed, radio shows hired "soundmen." These technicians used common objects to improvise noises, which brought the action of a story to life.

Here are a few more classic radio tricks for you to try.

Sprinkle rice on metal.

Tap a metal lid.

Stab a watermelon.

Crunch kitty litter.

8 make a floating finger

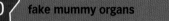

Think your eyes are playing tricks on you? You're right. As both of your eyes focus on your fingers, their paths of vision converge at one point. But then your eyes must make their paths of vision nearly parallel to focus on a distant object. While both your eyes can still see your fingertips, they see slightly overlapped images. This illusion is called a trick of perspective.

10 fake mummy organs

Before placing deceased love ones in sarcophagi, Ancient Egyptians would "mummify" them by wrapping their bodies in linen strips. They'd also remove some of the bodies' organs, which were then washed, dried, bandaged, and placed in special jars. It sure sounds like a lot of trouble, but the Egyptians believed that this process ensured a pleasant afterlife for the deceased.

29 dowse for water

People all around the world have practiced dowsing, also known as "water witching," for centuries. Dowsers claim to be able to locate water, oil, mineral deposits, and even lost objects using their minds—and a stick that twitches when the goods are found. Is it for real? Scientists tend to say no, but farmers and miners around the world continue to pay top dollar for dowsers' services.

read a love line

To read a friend's palm, start with her dominant hand (the hand she writes with). The lines on this hand will show you behaviors and attitudes that are firmly set in this person, as well as her past actions. Next read her other hand (the passive hand). These lines will tell you her potential in the future. Remember, palm reading is just for fun—don't take it too seriously!

squeeze an egg into a bottle

How does this trick work? When the lit match heats up the air in the bottle, the air molecules move around and spread apart. When the fire goes out, the molecules cool down and move closer together. Normally, this would suck in air from outside, but the egg blocks the entry. The pressure of the air molecules outside the bottle is so great that it forces the egg into the bottle.

fight a marshmallow war

Can't find these exact marshmallow creatures in your local grocery store? No worries—you can make your own 'mallow monsters. Stack a few marshmallows and outfit them with cheese crackers or sandwich sticks. Then let them fight it out in the microwave.

bend water with static

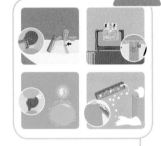

Everything in the world is made of atoms, and atoms are made of positive, negative, and neutral electric charges. These are known as protons (positive), electrons (negative), and neutrons (neutral). When certain objects, like your hair and a comb, come in contact, the electrons jump from one to the other. This leads to a buildup of negative charges on one object—in this case, on the comb.

Because opposites attract, these electrons will be drawn to positive charges (a state called static electricity). That's why the electrons on the negatively charged comb can tug other positively charged objects (like the torn tissue or stream of water) toward the comb. This attraction is also why the electrons on the television screen can jump to the tinfoil and why the electrons move from the balloon to the lightbulb: these negative charges want to take over positively charged areas! And when they do, the static electricity they generate can set off sparks or even make a little music.

Want to try one more static trick? Use static to separate salt and pepper! Make a small pile of salt and pepper on a flat surface. Rub a balloon vigorously against a wool sweater, then slowly bring the balloon near the salt and pepper pile—the pepper will fly up and stick to the balloon, leaving the salt.

master the angus spin

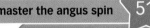

When you try this move, you may look like an idiot—but you'll be in good company! The invention of the Angus Spin is credited to vaudeville performer Curly Howard, one of the original Three Stooges. The move became a part of rock 'n' roll history when it was adopted by Angus Young of the band AC/DC (thus earning its name). Homer Simpson is another famous practitioner.

58 tell time with a potato

The acid in a potato is conductive, meaning electrically charged atoms can move around easily inside it. As the potato's acid eats away at the nail's zinc, a chemical reaction attracts electrons from the copper wire. The easiest way for these copper electrons to get to the nail is through the wires you've clamped on. The flow of these electrons is the electricity that powers the clock.

61 lift a friend's fingerprint

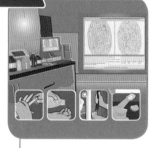
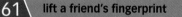

For more than a thousand years, people have known that fingerprints are special. In ninth-century China, businesspeople put their stamped fingerprints on documents instead of their signatures. By the 1500s, scientists had figured out that no two people had the same fingerprint. Even still, it wasn't until 1892 that the first criminal was caught as a result of fingerprint identification.

63 encode notes with a scytale

This spy device (pronounced "skee-ta-lee") was invented by the Ancient Romans for use during war. Each general had an identical rod and would write messages on leather strips wound around the rod, then unwind the strips and send them with a messenger. If the messenger carrying the unwound strips was captured, the message would be hard for the enemy to read. Sneaky!

64 send secrets by morse code

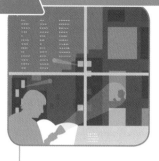

In the days before phones and radio, it could take people months to send a message across a long distance. In 1844, Samuel Morse popularized the telegraph, a device for sending electric signals across miles of cable. Messages were written in Morse code, a system of dots and dashes that symbolize letters and punctuation. It was very handy during World Wars I and II.

66 write in invisible ink

You can write disappearing messages with other common liquids that have been diluted with water, including milk, honey, vinegar, and even pee! Spies used all of these methods in a pinch during World Wars I and II, and may continue their use today. If you have a black light handy, you can also reveal invisible messages written in milk, liquid soap, or laundry detergent.

67 turn the world upside down

This device is also known as a camera obscura. Why does the image flip upside down, exactly? As light passes through the tiny hole, the light that is coming up from the bottom of the scene continues going up and the light shining down from the top of the scene continues traveling down. These separate light waves hit the paper screen, and the top and bottom are reversed.

Sun prints are also known as cyanotypes (cyan is a deep shade of blue). The paper is coated in a chemical that turns blue after exposure to sunlight. By placing objects over parts of the paper, you block the sunlight from reaching the surface beneath them, so those parts don't turn blue. When you wash the chemicals off with water, the parts of the chemical that didn't turn blue are washed away, and the paper gets bluer as it dries. Cyanotypes, invented in 1842, were popular with engineers and architects, who needed to reproduce notes and plans in the days before copy machines. They called their cyanotypes "blueprints."

You can make beautiful sun prints by cutting shapes out of thick paper and arranging them into scenes.

What causes this awesome explosion, you ask? When vinegar, which is an acid, combines with baking soda, a base, the resulting chemical reaction creates carbon dioxide gas. As the gas tries to rise into the air, it gets caught in the murky red liquid inside the volcano, creating foamy red bubbles. These gas-filled bubbles tumble out, erupting like lava from a volcano.

While marbleizing your masterpiece, did you see how the paint floats on top of the water instead of mixing into it or sinking? That's because water is denser than paint. The atoms of water are packed together tightly, while oil paint's atoms are held together more loosely.

Now that you know how marbleizing works, here are a few advanced techniques for you to try.

Blow across the paint's surface with a drinking straw. Try changing your angle and position for different designs.

Drag a feather across the paint for hundreds of tiny, delicate lines, or use a large fork to make bolder lines.

Remove leftover paint by drawing newspaper strips across the water. Add more paint and start again.

Spanish for "perforated paper," this festive artwork originates in Mexico, where it's hung up during religious, national, and family celebrations. Experienced artists there make designs by laying out a thick stack of tissue papers, setting down a stencil, then whacking a chisel through the papers with a mallet. Their designs usually feature birds, flowers, skeletons, or lattice patterns.

87 paste up a piñata

Think you might want to keep your piñata rather than bust it open? Then you'll need to adjust your papier-mâché recipe beforehand to keep the piñata from sprouting mold—gross! Mix one part flour with two parts water to get a thick, gluey consistency. Add more flour if it seems runny, or more water if it's too thick to dip the paper in. Then mix in 4 tbsp salt.

104 draw awesome manga

Manga are Japanese comics that have attracted avid fans of all ages from across the globe. Like novels, manga can be written about almost any subject, from medieval warfare to modern romance. Although manga originally appeared in Japan after World War II, their roots as an artform go back to the 1700s, and today manga are written by artists around the world.

114 ink a fake tattoo

Humans have tattooed themselves since prehistoric times—the tradition is thought to be more than 12,000 years old. The oldest mummy ever found in Europe, Otzi the Iceman (who lived way back around 4,000 BC), was found to have fifty-seven tattoos. Back then ink or soot was poked into the skin with a stick or rubbed into a design cut into the skin. Ouch!

118 screen-print a t-shirt

Screen-printing is sometimes called silk-screening. That's because when the Chinese first popularized this artform during the Song Dynasty (960–1279 AD), they used screens made of silk to transfer their images. Now we use polyester screens.

Here are some screen-printing tips.

 Simplify multiple tones into bold, high-contrast shapes.

 Use halftone dots to show gradual shifts in tone.

Avoid using thin lines, which can clog and smear easily.

 Avoid very large areas of solid color where ink might pool.

Print colors one at a time. Layer them for a cool effect.

122 make a magnetic compass

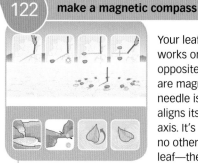

Your leaf-and-needle compass works on a familiar premise: that opposites attract. The Earth's poles are magnetized, so the magnetized needle is attracted to them and aligns itself with the north-south axis. It's important that there are no other magnetized items near the leaf—they can interfere with your compass's reading. It also helps to keep the leaf out of the wind.

collect water in damp sand 129

Even in desertlike areas that appear totally dry, water seeps into the ground during rains. The heat and sun warm only the ground's surface, and below the surface, the water never evaporates. When you dig your miniwell below this saturation point, water will slowly seep into the hole, seeking equilibrium. Remember, don't drink collected water unless you strain and boil it.

identify clouds 131

Earth isn't the only place with clouds. These atmospheric features also appear over all the other planets, with the exception of Mercury. Jupiter and Saturn have some clouds made of water, just like ours, but most of the other planets in the solar system have clouds made up of highly poisonous gases. Think of that next time you're bummed about a cloudy day!

blaze a trail 133

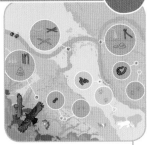

This trail-marking system has been around for a while. It's based on similar codes first invented by the San Bushmen in the Kalahari Desert to communicate silently while on trails. More recently, pioneers and hikers relied on them to mark (or blaze) new trails in the days before GPS, using painted symbols, flags, stone piles, or arranged sticks to point others in the right direction.

build a bat house 139

Bats, when they're not living in caves, prefer to sleep and raise young in trees—ideally in a space where bark has split off from a tree trunk. Deforestation means many bats have nowhere to live, so the best thing you can do for them is to offer a warm, secluded spot that mimics these tree homes. Your bat house should be tall and narrow, with a tiny entrance slot at the bottom and a scratchy interior surface that the bats can climb up and cling to.

So why go to all this trouble for these little critters? A bat eats hundreds, sometimes thousands, of bugs per hour, keeping your backyard free from pests that munch on your plants. Plus, bats are pollinators, which means they spread pollen between plants, causing new plants to grow that other creatures can then eat. So these dark-winged critters play a crucial part in our ecosystem: when bat populations decline, other local creatures will suffer as well.

While premade bat houses are available at garden stores and online, making them isn't hard. Our instructions are a good start; you can also check with a local conservation group to find out what cribs will be popular with your local bats.

make a hive for mason bees 142

Unlike common honeybees, Mason bees don't make honey, live in hives, or work together—each bee flies solo. They make their own private homes, usually in hollow reeds or small holes in wood. Although they won't make you any honey, Mason bees will come in very handy in your garden. Like bats, they're excellent pollinators, carrying pollen from flower to flower.

147 nurture tadpoles

When raising your tadpoles, don't overcrowd your tank. Each tadpole needs a gallon (3¾ l) of water. After a few weeks, the tadpoles will stop eating the food you give them, and their tails will start to disappear. Don't freak out! This means they are growing fine. As soon as little legs appear, place some large rocks in the tank so the tadpoles can climb out of the water to breathe.

148 cultivate carnivorous plants

Carnivorous plants use various methods of trapping insects, from the dramatic snap of the Venus flytrap to the drowning pool of the pitcher plant to the more common (but less exciting) sticky leaves of the "flypaper" plants. These plants are very ancient. They probably first appeared in the Early Cretaceous Period (145 million years ago), when dinosaurs roamed the Earth.

164 build a jiggly city

If you'd like to make your buildings more transparent, use more gelatin and less colored dessert mix. This extra gelatin will also help your creations stand up firmly on their own. When removing the "buildings" from their molds, turn them over and shake gently—a slapping sound means that they're ready to come out. If you don't hear it, let the molds set a little while longer.

166 bake stained-glass cookies

Want to make these cookies from scratch? You can skip the store-bought stuff and make the cookie dough at home with an adult using this easy recipe.

1½ c (350 g) butter, softened
2 c (400 g) white sugar
4 eggs
1 tsp vanilla extract
5 c (700 g) all-purpose flour
2 tsp baking powder
2 tsp salt

In a large bowl, mix the butter and sugar together until smooth. Beat in the eggs and vanilla. Add the flour, baking powder, and salt, then mix thoroughly. Cover, and leave dough in the fridge for 1 hour or longer.

Preheat the oven to 400°F (200°C). Sprinkle flour and a little sugar on a surface, then roll out the dough until it measures ½ in (1¼ cm) thick.

Follow the illustrated steps for cutting out the shapes, adding the crushed candy, and cooking the cookies. If you use the recipe here, you should need between 30 and 40 candies (150–200 g). After the cookies have baked, let them cool before eating—the "glass" will be very hot!

169 fold fortune cookies

These famous after-dinner treats are served in Chinese restaurants throughout the Western world, but they aren't Chinese at all. Several bakers in the U.S. state of California claimed to have invented the delicate cookies around the turn of the nineteenth century, and some theories trace their inspiration to either Chinese mooncakes or Japanese *sembei* crackers.

If you're feeling really gourmet, go ahead and make the filling for your tortellini yourself! Here are two simple, delicious recipes for cheese-and-veggie filling.

Basil-Ricotta Filling
1 c (225 g) part-skim ricotta cheese
3 tbsp Parmesan cheese, grated
3 basil leaves, finely chopped
2 pinches salt

Combine the ricotta, Parmesan, basil, and salt in a small bowl, then mix well. Cover and refrigerate, or fold into the tortellini immediately.

basil

Spinach-Ricotta Filling
1 c (225 g) mozzarella, shredded
¾ c (265 g) bread crumbs
2 eggs
10 oz (230 g) frozen spinach
1 c (235 g) ricotta cheese
1 clove garlic, chopped

spinach

Thaw and drain the spinach. Put all the ingredients into a food processor and blend until smooth. If the mixture is dry, add more egg; if it seems runny, add a few more bread crumbs. Cover and refrigerate, or add to the tortellini at once.

The rules shown here are from a version of the game called open bocce. Because this game has been popular all over the world since the time of the Ancient Romans, there are plenty of small, international variations. So when you travel, be sure to try *pétanque* or *boules* in France, bowls in England, *bolas criollas* in Venezuela, and *klootschieten* in the Netherlands.

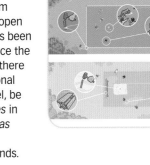

Horseshoes is another game with roots in Ancient Rome; it is probably based on the Olympic sport of discus. It was a popular pastime for soldiers during many wars, including the American Revolutionary War. When soldiers went home, horseshoes became a family game, then an official sport with famous players. Horseshoes is related to the Scottish game of quoits.

Plants breathe using a process called transpiration. In the case of celery, the plant "inhales" water through tiny canals in its stem called xylem and then "exhales" the water through pores in its leaves. When the celery sucks up dyed water, the xylem absorbs some dye from the water. Transpiration keeps the plant cool and transfers nutrients from its roots through its stalk and leaves.

The word "ninja" is derived from a Japanese word meaning "stealthy." As you might expect, the history of these ancient, secretive, and deadly warriors is tough to pin down! In ancient Japan, both boys and girls trained to be ninjas. One favorite trick was to wear sandals with bottoms carved to look like animal prints so that the ninja could sneak around without leaving footprints.

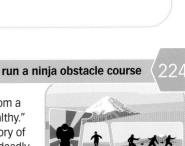

index

about the authors

Sarah Hines Stephens first learned to cook in order to get out of doing the dishes, and she still prefers making messes to cleaning them. One of three creative sisters, Sarah hails from generations of do-it-yourselfers: quilters, artists, writers, and gardeners. When Sarah is not facilitating semiexplosive science experiments and kid-friendly crafts, she writes books for kids. She has written more than sixty books. She lives with her husband and two children in a home filled with glitter, fabric scraps, glue, and power tools.

Bethany Mann is Sarah's sister and partner in creative mess-making. With a rallying cry of, "Hey, we could totally make that ourselves!" she has fearlessly led her family and friends in numerous craft adventures. These days Bethany channels her artistic powers for good by using recycled materials and growing vegetables. Her projects have been featured in craft books for adults and on DIY TV. She lives with her husband, teenage son, and a menagerie of rescued pets in the mountains near Santa Cruz, California. Read her blog at www.bitterbettyindustries.blogspot.com.

BONNIER PUBLISHING

Group Publisher John Owen

WELDON OWEN INC.

CEO, President Terry Newell

Senior VP, International Sales Stuart Laurence

VP, Sales and New Business Development Amy Kaneko

VP, Publisher Roger Shaw

VP, Creative Director Gaye Allen

Associate Creative Director Kelly Booth

Executive Editor Mariah Bear

Associate Editor Lucie Parker

Project Editor Frances Reade

Senior Designer Stephanie Tang

Designer Delbarr Moradi

Illustration Coordinator Sheila Masson

Production Director Chris Hemesath

Production Manager Michelle Duggan

Color Manager Teri Bell

Published in North America by
Candlewick Press
99 Dover Street
Somerville, Massachusetts 02144

Visit us at www.candlewick.com.

First edition 2009

Library of Congress Cataloging-in-Publication Data

Hines-Stephens, Sarah

 Show off : how to do absolutely everything one step at a time / Sarah Hines Stephens and Bethany Mann. — 1st ed.

  p. cm.

  ISBN 978-0-7636-4599-1

1. Recreation—Juvenile literature. 2. Amusements—Juvenile literature. 3. Handicraft—Juvenile literature. 4. Creative activities and seat work—Juvenile literature. I. Mann, Bethany. II. Title.

 GV182.9.H56 2009

 790.1'922—dc22   2009015847

10 9 8 7 6 5 4 3 2 1

Printed in China by SNP Leefung

Typeset in Vectora LH

A Show Me Now Book.
Show Me Now is a trademark
of Weldon Owen Inc.

Special thanks to:

Storyboarders

Esy Casey, Julumarie Joy Cornista, Sarah Lynn Duncan, Chris Hall, Paula Rogers, Jamie Spinello, Brandi Valenza

Illustration specialists

Hayden Foell, Raymond Larrett, Ross Sublett

Editorial and research support team

Marc Caswell, Mollie Church, Elizabeth Dougherty, Kat Engh, Alex Eros, Justin Goers, Emelie Griffin, Sarah Gurman, Susan Jonaitis, Peter Masiak, Grace Newell, Jennifer Newens, Paul Ozzello, Ben Rosenberg, Hiya Swanhuyser

Kid-reviewer panel

Emma Arlen, Leah Cohen, Sally Elton, Whitman Hall, Tesserae Honor, Nami Kaneko, Emily Newell, Eloise Shaw, Georgia Shaw

Illustration credits

Front cover

Liberum Donum (Juan Calle, Santiago Calle, Andres Penagos): bodysurfer, gymnast on high bar Vincent Perea: tattoo designs Bryon Thompson: cyclist, diver Otis Thomson: go-kart Gabhor Utomo: guitarist, punk girl Tina Cash Walsh: back walkover

Back cover

Joshua Kemble: robot Liberum Donum: vault Gabhor Utomo: barracuda

Key: bg = background; bd = border; fr = frames; ex = extra art

Kelly Booth: 30–32 Henry Boyle: 115 Esy Casey: 70 bg Hayden Foell: 23 bd, 24 bd, 36 bg, 38, 144, 163 ex Britt Hanson: 18–21, 23–25 bg, 34, 35 bg, 43–44, 54–57, 64, 67, 74, 89, 93, 100, 112, 143, 153–156, 160 bg, 176, 179, 196 bg, 197–198 Gary Henricks: 78, 90 Joshua Kemble: 76, 152, 175 fr, 203–204 Vic Kulihin: 37, 39 fr, 41, 75, 79–80, 116, 223, 224 Raymond Larrett: 26–29, 33, 35 fr, 36 fr, 59–60, 72, 81–82, 86, 88, 166 Liberum Donum: 1–4, 11, 15–17, 39 ex, 40, 42, 52, 58, 73, 101–104, 107, 113, 133–134, 147 fr, 158, 159 fr, 161, 164–165, 184, 188 bg, 189 bg, 190 bg, 199–200, 205–206, 212–213, 217–219 Christine Meighan: 5, 23, 83–84, 92,

162–163, 180, 182–183, 188 fr, 189 fr, 190 fr Hank Osuna: 160 fr, 177–178 Vincent Perea: 9–10, 68, 114, 135, 137–138, 148 Ross Sublett: 111 bg, 113 bg, 141 fr Bryon Thompson: 53, 98–99, 106, 120, 127, 139–142, 167–172, 191–194, 207–209, 220–221 Otis Thomson: 105, 186–187 Wil Tirion: 123, 126 Taylor Tucek: 70–71, 117 Gabhor Utomo: 7–8, 12–14, 22, 45–51, 61–63, 65–66, 69, 77, 85, 87, 91, 94–95, 108–110 bg, 118, 119 bg, 122, 124–125, 128–132, 145–146, 147 bg, 175 bg, 185, 201–202, 210–211 Tina Cash Walsh: 24 fr, 25 fr, 96–97, 108–110 fr, 111 fr, 119 fr, 136, 149–151, 157, 159 bg, 173–174, 181, 195–196 fr, 214–216, 222 Mary Zins: 6, 121

get involved!

SHOW ME TEAM

your picture here!

Want to be world famous? We probably can't help. But if you'd like to see your name in a book and show the world how smart, talented, or just plain weird you are . . . that we can do. Is there something that you think should have been in this book? Something you or your friends know how to do really well and want to show off? If so, we want to hear about it! Send us your best ideas, along with photos or video of you showing them off, and you could be featured in the next **Show Off** book.

www.showoffbook.com

ATTN: SHOW ME TEAM
Weldon Owen Inc.
415 Jackson Street
San Francisco, California 94111